HEBREW
AND
MODERNITY

HEBREW
AND
MODERNITY

Robert Alter

INDIANA UNIVERSITY PRESS
Bloomington and Indianapolis

The paper used in this publication meets the minimum requirements of American National Standard for Information Sciences—Permanence of Paper for Printed Library Materials, ANSI Z39.48-1984.

Manufactured in the United States of America

Library of Congress Cataloging-in-Publication Data

Alter, Robert.
    Hebrew and modernity / Robert Alter.
        p.   cm.
    Includes bibliographical references and index.
    ISBN 0-253-30473-3 (alk. paper). — ISBN 0-253-20856-4 (pbk.)
    1. Hebrew literature, Modern—History and criticism.   2. Israeli literature—History and criticism.   I. Title.
    PJ5017.A42   1994
    892.4'09—dc20   93-25423

1   2   3   4   5   99   98   97   96   95   94

*f*or Benjamin Harshav
who shares these exotic enthusiasms
and has finely illuminated their general interest

Contents

Preface

The essays collected in this volume, which were written from 1981 to 1993, propose a double set of continuities for the understanding of modern Hebrew literature: first, between the modern literature and the very long literary tradition that preceded it, and then between the literature of contemporary Israel and the century and a half of varied literary activity in Hebrew on European soil that antedated the creation of a Hebrew vernacular culture in Palestine. There are obviously crucial distinctions to be made between these two respective later phases of the literature and the antecedents on which they drew, as I try to explain, but the continuing relevance of the antecedents needs to be kept in mind. During the period when these essays were written, increasing attention has been devoted in America by readers and critics to Israeli literature, which has become abundantly available in English translation. This attention is partly justified by intrinsic literary worth—the Israeli novel, for example, seems to have entered a "boom" phase vaguely reminiscent of the Latin American novel a couple of decades ago—and is partly the consequence of the disproportionate fascination of Americans, especially Jewish Americans, with Israel. But the interest in Israeli literature, not only in America but in France, Italy, and elsewhere, is accompanied by certain misperceptions about its character. Few readers outside Israel are aware of the vigorous presence of a modern Hebrew literature in Europe before the dawn of Zionism that made both Zionism and the Hebrew culture of Israel possible. And since translations, even deft ones, tend to regularize and flatten the knotty distinctiveness of the original texts, the linguistic vitality and stylistic peculiarities of the Hebrew remain invisible to readers of English versions. Hebrew literature today is not merely a Colombian or Peruvian literature written in the Middle East in a Semitic language, but has its own abiding oddness, its own distinctive cultural problematic. What I have tried to do here is to highlight those elements of distinctiveness, in part by rendering an account of modern Hebrew literature as an evolving tradition from the eighteenth century to the present.

These essays were written for various occasions, but in sorting them out, I was happy to discover that the contours of a large historical picture began to emerge from them. Thus, I start with a piece that seeks to explain the fascinating anomalies of modern Hebrew literature from its inception to the present. There follow discussions of the relation of secular poetry in modern Hebrew to the millennia-old tradition of Hebrew verse; of the evolution of a viable language for realistic fiction in Hebrew; of relatively early experiments in Hebrew introspective writing and prose fiction in Europe and America; of the development of the Israeli novel through the first four decades of statehood; and of the response to the Holocaust in Hebrew poetry. The last four essays are considerations of individual writers, one of Yehuda Amichai, the leading Israeli poet, and three involving S. Y. Agnon, the major modern Hebrew novelist.

Four of these essays were originally published in *Commentary*, and single essays first appeared in *The New York Times Magazine*, *The Tel-Aviv Review*, *Prooftexts*, and in a volume called *The Legacy of Jewish Migration*, and I thank the editors of all those publications for their willingness to let me use the material here. The essay on Agnon's *Shira* was originally the afterword to the English translation of that novel, and I am grateful to Schocken Books for allowing me to reprint the piece. The inclusion of one item needs special explanation. In 1988, shortly before the appearance of my short book, *The Invention of Hebrew Prose*, I prepared for *Commentary* an article on the subject, about half of which was drawn from the introduction of the book, with the other half a kind of summary of the book's argument. I wanted to include it in the present volume because it fills in an important area of the big literary-historical picture and thus contributes to making this a book with a core of coherent argument instead of merely an assemblage of miscellaneous essays. I also must say that

The Invention of Hebrew Prose seems to have reached very few readers beyond the handful of specialists in the field, so there is some justification for making available here a précis of its attempt to trace the
history of modern Hebrew style. My thanks to the Washington University Press for permission to use material from the introduction to
Invention in the essay in this volume. Finally, two essays here appear
in print for the first time—the lead essay and the piece on Agnon's
psychological realism.

Secretarial and research expenses for this book were provided by
funds from the Class of 1937 Chair at the University of California at
Berkeley. Janet Livingstone, as always, prepared the typescript with
scrupulous care, bravely contending against the disorder of my own
crowded scrawl. I have stubbornly kept my own counsel in the interpretations and general overviews proposed here, but I owe a continuing debt of gratitude to the astute and devoted students of Hebrew literature I have been privileged to teach at Berkeley, and to my gifted
colleague in Hebrew and Comparative Literature, Chana Kronfeld.

HEBREW
AND
MODERNITY

HEBREW AND MODERNITY

The Yiddish novelist and poet Chaim Grade, in his remarkable memoir of his early years, *My Mother's Sabbath Days,* reports a curious — and providential — incident that casts instructive light on the peculiar role of Hebrew among Diaspora Jews as an undying dead language. As the Nazis moved into Lithuania in 1941, Grade fled eastward from Vilna into the Soviet Union, leaving his wife and mother behind, scarcely imagining what would be the fate of Jewish women and children as well as Jewish men under the German conquerors. He would soon discover that his own life in Russia hung by a frail thread that could easily be cut off by a whim of the military authorities. He is arrested en route on the suspicion of being a German spy. The main evidence against him is a pocket-size copy of the Hebrew Bible that the Red Army men find on his person. They are unwilling to believe it is what he claims, suspecting it may be part of his spy's paraphernalia or the equipment of a "German pastor" (perhaps mistaking the alien Hebrew characters for almost equally alien Gothic ones). Grade is sent off in the company of three soldiers, ostensibly to the local headquarters, but more probably, he fears, judging by the tenor of the soldiers' remarks to him, to be shot. As they reach a little meadow in the forest, an officer mounted on a brown horse comes galloping up to them at top speed and demands to know what is going on. One of the soldiers hands him

Grade's passport together with the incriminating Bible. The officer leafs through it "with a bemused and somber expression," then hands it back to Grade together with the passport and peremptorily orders the release of the prisoner. Grade, suddenly left standing alone in the meadow, finds that the Bible is opened to Jeremiah and reads these words, which he seizes on as a talisman and prophecy: "For I am with thee, saith the Lord, to save thee: though I make a full end of all nations whither I have scattered thee, yet I will not make a full end of thee: but I will correct thee in measure, and I will not leave thee altogether unpunished."

A crucial act of communication has taken place here, though the circumstances throw a veil of ambiguity over its precise nature. The grateful Grade is convinced that the Red Army officer is a Jew. Minimally, this would mean that the Russian is able to identify the Hebrew characters of the Bible and recognize through them a secret solidarity with the arrested man bearing a Polish passport. But Grade is inclined to conclude that the mounted officer has actually understood the Hebrew text he has inspected, and that he has deliberately left the Bible open to the passage in Jeremiah as a message to the prisoner. If the officer, as seems plausible, were in his thirties or forties, he would have received his basic schooling in prerevolutionary Russia, and could easily have attended a ḥeder and yeshiva (as did Grade in Lithuania), or might even have undergone modern-style instruction in Hebrew as a classical and revived language. In the encounter in the forest, he is of course speaking Russian, and anything Grade may say to him is enunciated in his own version of foreign-accented Russian. Were they alone, they might well use Yiddish as a more comfortable lingua franca. In fact, the silent but saving communication between them is effected through the Hebrew words of the Bible. Perhaps the officer merely remembers the familiar square-letter typography, moving from right to left, of scriptural and liturgical texts from home rites and synagogue in a Jewish boyhood early in the century. It is tempting, though, and culturally quite feasible, to adopt Grade's inference that the officer knows his way around the Hebrew Bible and uses its words to convey to Grade a fraternal exhortation of the utmost urgency. The passage from Jeremiah, it should be noted, speaks of a national fate in dark times two-and-a-half millennia in the past, which is here presumed to be re-enacted, individually by Grade and collectively by the Jewish people, in these dire middle years of the twentieth century.

Grade's story suggests something about the flickering but intense half-life led by Hebrew for two thousand years even as Jews made themselves at home in Romance, Germanic, Slavic, Arabic, and other linguistic climates whether through dialect adaptations or by fully embracing the normative language of the surrounding culture. One can find only approximate and incomplete analogies for the peculiar, stubbornly persistent diglossia perpetuated by Diaspora Jewry, and this condition was bound to give a special spin to the literature created in Hebrew in the modern period, at least until the "normalization" of the language in Israel and sometimes – for a literature never entirely discards its own antecedents – even afterward. In the mouth of Yiddish-speaking Jews, Hebrew was *loshn koydesh*, Holy Tongue, a designation that might imply a certain functional correspondence to Church Latin and the concomitant use of Latin as the language of a learned elite. A full competence in reading and writing Hebrew was in fact the possession of the Jewish clerical class – rabbis, cantors, ritual slaughterers, circumcisers, scribes – as well as of those who had undergone higher talmudic education and then entered other professions. But because Judaism is not an ecclesiastical religion, Hebrew also suffused the ordinary home through daily and weekly and festival ritual, and many Jews who were not part of any intellectual elite had at least a smattering of the language, sometimes sufficient to stumble their way in near comprehension through the simpler biblical, rabbinic, and liturgic texts. Moreover, even beyond the orbit of the sundry revivals of the language as an explicitly literary medium from the tenth century to the twentieth, written Hebrew continued to serve certain secular purposes, in community chronicles, travel books, family records, personal and business correspondence, and other kinds of texts. All this suggests that it was less wildly improbable than one might at first imagine for small groups of Yiddish-speaking nineteenth-century Jews in the Austro-Hungarian and Russian Empires to adopt Hebrew as the medium for essays, poems, treatises of popular science, autobiography, and prose fiction. It also suggests that there were likely to be some abiding peculiarities in the literature they created.

Obviously, Hebrew is in many fundamental ways a literature just like any other literature, only written in strange letters and read from right to left. But the anomalies of its cultural matrix generate at least some distinctive features, providing both special expressive resources and limitations of expression as well as a nuance of distinctive orientation toward the realm of modernity in which Hebrew writers have done their work. There are, I think, three underlying anomalies of modern Hebrew literature. The first is its polyglot contexts. Chaim Grade's anecdote might be taken as an emblem of this predicament: a communication that is carried out through Hebrew embedded in a Russian conversation for which Yiddish serves as an unspoken background, and of course conveyed retrospectively in a Yiddish narrative. The polyglot context meant that Hebrew was always in some way a *contested* language, compelled to emulate, outdo, and incorporate linguistic rivals. As we shall see, these pressures of the polyglot context have not entirely disappeared even in contemporary Israel, where Hebrew has become the undisputed dominant language. The second anomaly of Hebrew literature is its sheer longevity. Together with Sanskrit and Chinese, it is one of the three languages in the world in longest continuous literary use, with the lexicon and grammar of the earliest texts for the most part still perfectly understandable to literate modern readers and still usable by modern writers. This longevity provides immense resources for the writer, though on occasion it can also be a liability. Finally, the modern literary revival of Hebrew was intricately involved in a contest of ideologies, and though that aspect of Hebrew expression in the modern world has by and large receded from the contemporary Israeli scene, it still sometimes casts a shadow.

In regard to literary heteroglossia, the Russian theorist M. M. Bakhtin has made students of literature aware of how supposedly unitary languages are themselves made up of secondary languages reflecting class, region, profession, ideology, and much else. In his view, the literary text — especially since Rabelais and especially the novel — is a crowded arena of encounter in which the sundry languages of a culture clash, challenge each other, modify each other, and produce a complex dialogue. The polyglot nature of Hebrew texts might be thought of as an extreme instance of this general phenomenon, for with Hebrew, in the prevernacular European period, even before the writers had invented literary equivalents of what I have called the culture's secondary languages, the language so peculiarly elected for literary use was always implicitly challenged by and involved in dialogue with another language — at least Yiddish, in the earliest modern texts German, and later Russian and occasionally Polish.

The rebirth of a secular Hebrew literature in Andalusia in the late tenth century had occurred in a situation of literal (not Bakhtinian) diglossia: the new poets spoke Judeo-Arabic and used it as well for discursive writing while they composed their sumptuous poetry in Hebrew. But this was not, I think, felt to be a contested diglossia because it corresponded so closely to the linguistic situation of the surrounding Arabs, who spoke vernacular Arabic and wrote poetry in another, classical language, the Arabic of the Koran. If one genre of Hebrew strophic poetry actually introduced vernacular Arabic or Old Spanish in the concluding line, the *harjah*, this embedding of the spoken language in the literary one was an exact replication of the use of the *harjah* in the corresponding Arabic genre. After the Iberian tradition of secular Hebrew poetry is transplanted to Italy, instances of flaunted literary diglossia continue to occur — most flamboyantly, in the acrobatic performance of the poetic virtuosos who produce lines of Hebrew verse that could also be reread as transliterated Italian to yield a second meaning. It is hard to be certain about the implicit feel for languages of the poets, but my guess is that in Renaissance and baroque Italy, too, there was not a strong sense of contested diglossia because here, as well, in a country divided by mutually incomprehensible regional dialects, there existed a normative practice of speaking one language and writing another — literary Italian.

When, however, a self-consciously modernizing Hebrew literature emerged in Central and Eastern Europe, beginning in Enlightenment

Germany in the late eighteenth century, the linguistic circumstances had changed. In these regions, diglossia was not the general standard for literary expression: Schiller wrote his poetry in German, Gogol his fiction in Russian, each using his mother tongue. The sharp difference for Hebrew writers was that their mother tongue, *mama loshn,* was Yiddish; their immediate models of literary emulation were in a European language, usually Russian; and yet they composed their works in Hebrew, a language that nobody, themselves included, as yet spoke. The unvoiced question hovering over every modern Hebrew text at least until after the First World War was: Why of all tongues Hebrew, when other, more natural alternatives beckoned?

The response of Hebrew writers to this challenge of diglossia was at first clumsy but in the end brilliantly resourceful. The poetry and prose of the Haskalah, the Hebrew Enlightenment (schematically, from 1783, the year that the first Hebrew journal began publication, to 1881, the beginning of the mass pogroms in Russia) was a stiff brocade of phrases woven from mostly biblical sources. Oddly and instructively, though the verbal materials were indigenous, and for the most part scrupulously maintained as such in the zealous purism of the writers' Hebraism, the overall stylistic effect was a little foreign. This paradox is, I suspect, a consequence of the fact that Haskalah writers ransacked the classic Hebrew sources in the earnest, perhaps sometimes anxious aim of creating a Hebrew equivalent of European sublime poetry and decorous prose. In the self-consciousness of this particular mode of literary diglossia, the language of the text is puristically Hebrew, but one senses the shadow presence of a second language on which Hebrew, with its different lexicon, syntax, grammar, and associations, is imperfectly mapped. To speculate on the psychology of this linguistic predicament, the writers seem actuated by a sense of superiority regarding the language they are using, which is after all, the Eternal Tongue, and by a sense of inferiority in relation to the European literary models they are struggling to emulate.

By the first two or three decades after the end of the Haskalah, Hebrew writers were finding ways to live at creative ease with their condition of diglossia. In prose, the celebrated turning point was the exemplary career of S. Y. Abramowitz, who after an initial Hebrew novel in the Haskalah manner, switched to Yiddish and made himself the first modern master of Yiddish prose. After twenty years of such activity, he began, in 1886, to write stories again in Hebrew and, more significantly, to rework his major Yiddish novels into Hebrew. Abramowitz's basic strategy was to exploit the internal, "Bakhtinian" heteroglossia of Hebrew by producing a lively, often comic interplay in his texts of the sundry historical strata of the Hebrew language. Though he emulated aspects of Cervantes, Gogol, and Dickens, the linguistic other in his Hebrew fiction is Yiddish, which is felt not as a shadow presence but as a pungent, tonally rich language for which he creates, through the most surprising combinations of witty allusion and lexical fecundity, persuasive Hebrew equivalents. The next generation of Hebrew prose writers, around the turn of the century, took an opposite tack, using many of the linguistic resources Abramowitz had uncovered but also pulling and stretching and fracturing the indigenous patterns of the language to make it effectively cover a European semantic map.

Though common sense might conclude that this polyglot context of Hebrew literature would disappear with the migration of Hebrew from its anomalous European location, that has not entirely been the case. To begin with, Hebrew literature, though now created preponderantly in the Middle East, resolutely remains a Western literature, looking to formal and even sometimes stylistic models in English, German, and, to a lesser degree, Russian, French, and Spanish. On a more immediate level, Israel continues to be a country of spectacularly dense immigration. Hebrew is by now perfectly secure as the national language, but dozens of other languages are vociferously spoken, and there is even a daily press in a good many of them. A Hebrew writer in Israel is thus repeatedly confronted with languages that manifestly stake out a different semantic zone, carry a different freight of history and associations, from the writer's own language. It is noteworthy that in the youngest generation of Hebrew writers, the fiction of David Grossman and Yehudit Katzir should incorporate untranslated Yiddish — snippets in Grossman's novel *See Under: Love*, whole pas-

sages in Katzir's novella "Fellini's Shoes" — and that another new Israeli writer, Yoel Hoffman, should create, in his avant-garde mode, aggressively polyglot texts. This instance of Hoffman, whose first book
was published as recently as 1989, is worth pausing over briefly.

The human population of Hoffman's intermittently narrative,
quasi-lyric texts, with their frequent excursuses in flashback and fantasy to the prewar European past, is chiefly the immigrants to Israel
from Central and Eastern Europe. He repeatedly allows them to speak
in their own languages, embedding the foreign words and sentences in
his Hebrew texts in Hebrew transliteration. This procedure is accompanied by a peculiar typographical device. The books are laid out with
wide margins (and two of his three books are printed on one side of the
page only), with Hebrew translations of the foreign-language terms
provided in the margins, in smaller type. In his 1991 *The Book of Joseph*, the languages introduced in this fashion are German and Yiddish
(by far the two most frequent), Hungarian, Arabic, English, plus a sam-
ple of Berlin dialect. In Hoffman's fiction, the polyglot context of
modern Hebrew literature conspicuously becomes polyglot text. Now,
polyglot literary texts are not uncommon in European modernism, as
any English reader, recalling Joyce, Pound, and Eliot, will recognize.
For the Anglophone and Continental writers, however, the polyglot
text crystallizes the idea of a multivoiced concert of European culture.
Thus, in *The Waste Land*, English is of course the medium of expression, or if one prefers, the framing language of the poem, but it addresses and is addressed by the embedded representatives of Greek,
Latin, Sanskrit, Italian, German, and French. Taken together, they constitute a single Indo-European cultural tradition in multiple accents
and local habitations, and both the legacy of values and the modern
spiritual crisis that are the poem's subject are their common possession.

In Yoel Hoffman's polyglot texts, on the other hand, there seems to
be little sense of a common cultural legacy. On the contrary, the way
he presents his foreign languages conveys a feeling of their stubborn
otherness to Hebrew, and of Hebrew to them. The decision to provide
marginal translations is more a literary strategy than a practical aid to

the reader, as one may infer from the limit case of very simple utterances in English or Yiddish: it is hard to imagine that an Israeli reader likely to pick up an avant-garde text of this sort would not have enough English to understand "It is raining" or enough Yiddish to understand *geh avek*. The procedure of transliteration compounds this sense of the otherness of different languages, for even if, say, you understand German, you are obliged to labor arduously through the transliteration in order to reconstruct the German words actually spoken in the dialogue. (Again, the motive for using transliteration can hardly be a practical one, since that would assume, quite fantastically, that most Hebrew readers are incapable of processing words written in the Latin alphabet.) Hoffman's own Hebrew is a quietly fluent, nicely idiomatic literary middle diction, capable at moments of haunting poetic effects. Its use in a polyglot text extrudes, I would argue, the consciousness of Hebrew as a contested language which has clung to Hebrew writing since the eighteenth century. As one reads, one is aware of the author's Israeli Hebrew, which can say certain things very well, and one is simultaneously aware, for example, of the German spoken by the characters, redolent of Central European drawing rooms crowded with velvet-upholstered furniture and glass-doored bookcases, of beer halls, of Goethe and Heine. In this language, other things are said, and any bridges between the two linguistic-cultural realms are perilously rickety ones.

There is a poignant moment in *The Book of Joseph* that sharply illustrates this quandary of heteroglossia. The child protagonist of the first chapter has been brought to a kibbutz to live and is introduced to his prospective peer group. A teacher is talking to the children about what a leaf looks like under a magnifying glass. He asks the newcomer whether he knows what *photosyntesa* means. The child, who customarily speaks German with family-members and Hebrew with others, assumes this strange term must be German and automatically answers, *nein*. The kibbutz kids, who of course are monolingual, explode with mocking laughter. The incident is obviously a representation of the parochialism of Israeli society and its capacity – especially among the young – for cruelty to those who are different, but it also enacts the contest of languages in which Hebrew has repeatedly found itself. On one level, the baffled little boy is right: *photosyntesa* is not really a Hebrew word, the very act of linguistic loan serving as a token of Hebrew's continual struggle to equal the range and precision of its European counterparts, while the mockery of the children, who seize on *nein* as an idiot's syllable, of course cannot recognize it as a tiny fragment of a whole world, in its cultural otherness quite beyond the ken of their Hebrew monoligualism. Modern Hebrew creativity has often been manifested in a state of underlying tension with other languages, and the contemporary instance of Yoel Hoffman suggests that the tension is still profoundly experienced at least by some Hebrew writers.

The great literary longevity of Hebrew is, by and large, a less problematic defining feature of modern Hebrew literature. The dimension of longevity is more evident – indeed, it is ubiquitously felt – in the European phase of modern Hebrew literature, but, as I shall try to indicate, it has by no means disappeared from contemporary Israeli writing. For the European-based Hebrew writers, who achieved literary competence in the language not by hearing it spoken from childhood but by imbibing through early instruction the whole range of classic Hebrew sources, there was no way to write about anything, however personal or contemporary, except through the mediation of antecedent Hebrew literature. A twentieth-century English poet may recall English poetry of the past four centuries (earlier texts begin to be unassimilable) and may choose to allude to some of these predecessors. Yeats can invoke Blake, Frost can invoke Shakespeare, but these are selective allusions embedded in the secure matrix of their modern language with its colloquial background, Irish English and American English, respectively. An approximately contemporaneous poet writing in Hebrew, like H. N. Bialik (1873–1934), draws his entire language from three thousand years of continuous literary activity in Hebrew, much of which he probably knows by heart, with the oldest texts still as readily intelligible to him as Shakespeare is to Robert Frost. The literary effect of this ineluctable engagement in a long tradition is not easy to fathom for a reader unacquainted with Hebrew. First, it means that allusion is not an occasional or even frequent elective device but in many texts the woof and warp of the poem, from line to line and phrase to phrase, even from one grammatical form to another. I once heard Avraham Shlonsky, the leading figure in the generation of poets who rebelled against Bialik in the twenties and thirties, say in his characteristically theatrical manner that every Hebrew word came swirling behind it a wake three thousand years long, so that the poet had to struggle consciously to cut off echoes and associations he did not want in his poem. In contemporary Israel, where Hebrew literature again flourishes on a vernacular base after a hiatus of two thousand years, allusion is by no means so pervasive as it once was, but dialogue through allusion at least with the biblical layer of the past still occurs in a surprising range of texts, in both poetry and prose.

In the first years of this century, Bialik, then living in Odessa, wrote three extraordinary long poems, following the narrative generic model of the Russian *poema*—one a response of moral outrage to the Kishinev massacre of 1903; a second a powerful mythopoeic poem based on a talmudic legend about the generation of Israelites who died in the desert after the exodus; and a third a luminous, sensually mystical evocation of a child's primordial experience of unity with nature. All three poems, as might be expected, teem with allusions to Genesis, Exodus, Numbers, Psalms, Job, Isaiah, Jeremiah, the Song of Songs, Ecclesiastes, and much else in the Bible, not to speak of later Hebrew sources; and their terrific poetic density is scarcely imaginable without a detailed awareness of this background of allusion. What is equally instructive about the multilayered character of Hebrew literature in Europe is that the presence of this long literary tradition is also felt on the level of prosody, syntax, and the basic patterning of words. The *poemas* are cast in unrhymed hexameter lines, pronounced according to the Ashkenazic practice that places the accent for most words on the penultimate syllable. But, as the critic A. M. Lifshitz shrewdly pointed out in the 1930s, there is also a "hidden meter" in Bialik's poetry that is strictly biblical. Here, the accent for most words would fall on the last syllable, as it is in synagogue Torah reading, which follows the accent markings of the Masoretic text; and around the cesura dictated by the hexameter form, many lines end up in a pattern of semantically parallel utterances in each half of the line, usually accompanied by an equal number of accented syllables in each half-line – precisely the form of biblical poetry. The prophet Isaiah might have been puzzled by the nihilistic theology and the occasional postbiblical locutions of Bialik's *The Desert Dead*, but he would have had little difficulty grasping most of its language and appreciating its mastery of a poetic form familiar to him. In fact, the poem – prosodically, lexically, and conceptually – is a kind of palimpsest in which one stratum of Hebrew experience has been inscribed on top of another, the language of Job and Psalms overwritten with phrases and images from the Talmud, all of it limning a spiritual abyss which is perceived through an early twentieth-century sense of historical crisis.

The texture of Hebrew prose in the European period can be as densely allusive as that of the poetry. The exemplary instance of S. Y. Abramowitz is a case in point. But even when allusion is not crucial or abundant, the language woven out of age-old antecedents creates a kind of stylistic echo chamber, simultaneously embracing and artfully distancing its modern objects of representation. S. Y. Agnon (1888–1970), the undisputed master of modern Hebrew fiction, illustrates this paradoxical dynamic through the extremeness of his own stylistic practice. Early on, he adopted a beautifully synthesized distillation of the Hebrew of the rabbinic sages of Late Antiquity as the language of his novels and stories, and he almost never veered from this fundamental choice of stylization, even though he spent most of his adult life in Jerusalem with modern Hebrew spoken all around him. By and large, Agnon has not fared well in translation precisely because of the peculiarly Hebraic evocative power of his stylistic achievement. His symbolic inventiveness, his psychological insight, his shrewd perception of social milieu may be more or less visible in translation, but without the allusive music of his archaizing Hebrew, for which there is no viable equivalent in Western languages, the writing is liable to seem flat or even awkward. Let me offer a small characteristic example, where explicit allusion is not prominent, of this untranslatable echo play indigenous to the Hebrew tradition that culminates in Agnon's prose.

Hirshl Hurvitz, the protagonist of Agnon's 1935 novel, *A Simple Story*, stands forlorn in the rain at the garden gate of his lost love, Blume Nacht. I offer my own rather literal translation instead of Hillel Halkin's fluent, idiomatic English version which in its freedom with the original substitutes a modern American literary diction for Agnon's arch stylization:

> Silently, silently the rain fell. A veil is cast over all the world, and you don't even see yourself. But Blume's image rises up before you as on the day she stroked your head when you entered her room and she fled and came back. Hirshl rested his head on the handles of the bolt and began to weep. (Chap. 23)

In translation, these lines are quite unremarkable. In the Hebrew, the vocabulary and grammar are those of early rabbinic literature, though it must be said that the language also exhibits a *composed*, aesthetic character that owes more to a discipleship to Flaubert than to the Mishnah and Midrash. Thus, the first short sentence repeats a recurrent pattern in the novel of beginning passages with a doubled adjective ("silently" is actually adjectival in the Hebrew), and it also produces a nice onomatopoeic effect of dull drumming: *d'mumím d'mumím yardú hag'shamím.* The switch to second person and present tense — one of several different techniques Agnon uses for reporting inner experience — for the interior monologue picks up the quasi-colloquial nature of his rabbinic sources. Hirshl's anguish is meant to be very real, yet the language flaunts its archaic background. Instead of any of several words for "veil" current in modern Hebrew, Agnon uses the recondite Greek loanword *pruzma* redolent of the Talmud (the original meaning is "apron"), and another Greek loanword with similar talmudic midrashic associations, *ikonia,* for "image." And even on a sublexical level, instead of standard modern (and biblical) *'ein 'atah* for "you don't," he chooses the distinctively rabbinic *'i 'atah,* which has the odd effect of making Hirshl as he talks to himself

also sound like a fourth-century Galilean or Babylonian sage enunci-
ating a legal or exegetical principle. The only specific literary allusion
here is in the last sentence, where Hirshl's head – caressed in memory,
rain-soaked and sorrowing in actuality – rests "on the handles of the
bolt," a recollection of the phrase in the Song of Songs, when the beloved's perfumed hand reaches out to open the lock for her lover who
has gone. In any case, the quality that pervades the passage, and Agnon's prose in general, as well as a good deal of modern Hebrew writing in all genres, is not allusion but allusivity. The events of the novel
take place in a Galician town in the first decade of the twentieth century. The novelist's imagination of Hirshl's stymied psychosexual development is informed by Freudian notions of the unconscious and
the psychopathology of everyday life. But the language that conveys
all this is an odd affirmation of continuity with three millennia of Hebrew literature. The effect of this archaizing affirmation is hard to describe and is no doubt perceived differently by different Hebrew readers: in part, it bespeaks a classicizing, aesthetic impulse; in part, it
generates a sense of ironic distance between the language and the
world it purports to represent; in part, it is a declaration of allegiance
to the national literary tradition.

I have invoked Agnon as an extreme instance which in its very ex-
tremity lays bare a typical tendency. Contemporary Israeli writing, as
one would assume, more characteristically turns for its lexical and idiomatic norms to Hebrew as it is spoken formally and informally and
as it is written in the daily press. But that commonsensical assumption is only partly sustained by the literary evidence. To begin with,
Agnon, through the sheer power of his example, has exerted a certain
intermittent influence on later Hebrew prose, directly felt in the style
of a few writers, like A. B. Yehoshua, Aharon Appelfeld, and Yehuda
Amichai (in his fiction), and obliquely present in other writers –
minimally, in a surprising fondness for the occasional rabbinic locu-
tion in the midst of contemporary-sounding prose. The phenomenon
of generalized allusivity, however, is by no means limited to the influence of a single older stylist. Writers, after all, are by the dictates of
their art hypersensitive to their linguistic medium, which for Hebrew

means an acute awareness of the expressive possibilities, and the spiritual dangers, of exploiting words and phrases embedded in long past ages. Such awareness continues to make the texture of Hebrew writing in certain ways different from its contemporary counterparts elsewhere. Dan Pagis (1930–1986), a poet whose own work is on the whole very sparing in the use of allusion, shrewdly defines this peculiarity of the Hebrew medium in a posthumously published poem entitled "A Problem of Language":

The girl called Hebrew
is the last child of a very good family.
But you know what? She flits around.
Every day something else.
You can't count on her,
her word is no true word.
She's not even pretty: acne,
big feet. And she's shrill,
and stubborn as a mule.
And what's worse:
She doesn't allow whoever wants
to throttle her wild voice
and to give her a decent burial
in the double cave.

The poem's Hebrew is ostentatiously colloquial — in contrast to Pagis's general practice, which cultivates a poetic middle diction — and the use of colloquial language makes a certain thematic point: even the speaker of up-to-the-minute street Hebrew cannot escape the long history of the language. The only words here one would not hear in a Tel Aviv taxi or a Jerusalem living room are the last two of the poem, *me'arat hamakhpelah*. The double cave is the cave Abraham purchases from the Hittites in Genesis 23 to bury his dead. Words, unlike people, resist burial. A person who really works with them seriously, as does a Hebrew poet, is repeatedly confronted with their primordial past, their terrific momentum of associations generated in a world of theological and mythic and moral values alien to the poet, challenging him, sometimes perhaps subverting him. Pagis, whose native language was German and who read fluently all the Western European languages, would have been especially sensitive to how writing Hebrew differed in this one respect from writing another language. His image of a wild voice in the language that refuses to be throttled expresses, from the standpoint of a practicing poet, a notion that Gershom Scholem articulated as early as 1926 in what has recently become a celebrated text, addressed to the German Jewish theologian, Franz Rosenzweig. The revival of the Hebrew language, Scholem proposed, was in effect an act of playing with spiritual dynamite. Each Hebrew word concealed an "abyss" (German *Abgrund*, Hebrew *tehom*, a key word in both Scholem's languages). "Having conjured up the ancient names day after day, we can no longer suppress their potencies. We roused them, and they will manifest themselves." Many Hebrew writers in recent decades have made studied efforts to use the unadorned flatness of the quotidian language as a literary vehicle — the poetry of Natan Zach in the 1950s and afterward is a striking instance of this general impulse. But Scholem's point, and Pagis's, is that Hebrew refuses to be entirely subdued by the contemporary. I realize that my formulation, with a volitional verb attached to "Hebrew," attributes conscious agency to the language, but in this I am following the logic of Scholem and Pagis — a metaphoric logic that highlights the capacity of the ancient-modern language to preserve the semantic pressure of the millennia-old words that it continues to invoke.

The third anamolous condition of modern Hebrew literature is its originally ideological character. This does not at all mean that every modern Hebrew text of the European period articulates an ideological position. At least some writers, like the poet Avraham Ben Yitzhak Sonne and the poet and novelist David Fogel (both flourished in Vienna between the two wars) remained resolutely anti-ideological; and if a dedicated Zionist poet like Bialik could occasionally and regrettably produce poems that were mere versifications of Ahad Ha'am's cultural Zionism, much of his poetry is intensely personal, or treats national themes with an imaginative complexity that dissolves their ideological contours. The very choice of Hebrew, however, as a literary medium, unnatural as it was in the European setting of Yiddish-speaking Jews, involved an ideological affirmation. Hebraism, Yiddishism, Bundism, and in Germany, Reform Judaism and conscious assimilationism, were all efforts to redefine the Jewish condition under the exigencies of modernity – in the last limit-case of the instances I have enumerated, to "redefine" it by discarding it. Everyone of those refugees from the yeshiva world in Odessa, Vilna, Warsaw, Lemberg, and Vienna who sought to create secular poems and stories out of the Hebrew of sacred texts absorbed in early youth was implicitly declaring that from this point on Jewish culture would have a new meaning, would propel itself into a wholly new context of European modernity. Religion would no longer be the chief defining term of Jewish existence and Hebrew would no longer be the Holy Tongue presided over by a clerical class but rather the medium of a national culture.

This basic ideological commitment to the idea of a new Hebrew culture was capacious enough to embrace a variety of conflicting ideological trends – Enlightenment rationalism, Hebrew Nietzscheanism, neotraditionalism, aestheticism, and both political and cultural Zionism. It should also be said that like any ideology, Hebraism encouraged a range of dubious or exasperating cultural practices, involving certain simplifications and distortions of the Jewish past, a single-mindedness sometimes bordering on fanaticism, and in many instances a ruthlessness toward manifestations of Jewish life – Yiddish above all – that did not fit into its own agenda. The story of the revival of Hebrew, with its responses to rival ideologies and its grappling with problems like lexical innovation and the concoction of a new phonetics, is a fascinating episode in modern cultural history; it is told in detail with incisive authority by Benjamin Harshav in his recent book, *Language in Time of Revolution*. My own rapid overview will not pause for consideration of the intricate details, but suffice it to say that those details, as Harshav shows, in everything from the cultivation of certain literary styles and the embrace of certain genres to the development of theories about how and why the language should be spoken, reflect a concerted will on the part of an intellectual elite to effect a revolution in national life – reflect what I have called an ideological impulse. This ideological impulse is a direct consequence of the peculiar historical circumstances of modern Hebrew literature and should not be confused with the supposedly "collective, and even revolutionary, enunciation" that the French theorists Deleuze and Guattari attribute to all "minor literature," which in their muddled and pretentious manner they convert from a historical phenomenon to a metaphor for radical critique.

By 1948, when the State of Israel was established with Hebrew as its official language, the age of revolution was over. But as with much else in history, and perhaps especially Jewish history, one is inclined to add: more or less over. On the one hand, there is abundant and impressive evidence that the Zionist program of "normalization" has succeeded more in language and literature than in any other realm. Yaakov Shabtai's 1977 novel, *Past Continuous,* one of the most original achievements of the last few decades of Hebrew fiction, is a pivotal instance of the flourishing of literature outside the pale of old ideologies. Shabtai's supple, unostentatiously rich Hebrew is wrought on a matrix of colloquial usage. Some of his characters do have vehement political views, but these are part of the Israeli social realia he encompasses. He uses the language he has absorbed through all the normal cultural avenues to render a personal vision of life – in his case, in some of its bleakest aspects of loss and decline. There is no sense, however, that a cultural identity is at issue in the use of this particular language, that a position is being staked out through the instrument of Hebrew against other possible positions. An American friend of mine who closely follows Israeli literature in English translation astutely observed that *Past Continuous* was the first Israeli novel he had encountered in which Jewish national concerns were in no way at issue: the social materials of the novel are of course distinctively and authentically Israeli, but the interests of the book remain unselfconsciously universal.

The example of Shabtai may well be the dominant one for the future of Hebrew literature, but on the other hand, there is persistent evidence that the act of writing in Hebrew, at least for some novelists and poets and playwrights, is still not entirely disengaged from its ideological past, still implicitly involves a complicated argument on questions of national identity. One historically instructive illustration of this continuing ideological context was the critical flurry triggered in 1986 by the appearance of Anton Shammas's *Arabesques*, the first Hebrew novel written by an Arab. For the most part, the Israeli literary world warmly welcomed Shammas's entry as an Arab Israeli into the dominant national literature, but there was also a consciousness of having crossed a cultural watershed because writing in Hebrew was still associated in most people's minds, for good reason, with being Jewish and even with affirming a particular Jewish identity. The peculiarity of what is implied by Hebrew becomes evident if one compares the excited and perhaps ambivalent reception of *Arabesques* to the everyday occurrence in America of a writer from a linguistic minority or immigrant group switching to English – say, Joseph Brodsky from Russian to English. Here, no eyebrows are raised because the majority language is simply that, without a historical freight of ideological function.

One testimony to the continuing nexus between language and ideology is the recourse of several recent Israeli novels to what might be called a linguistic archeology of modern Hebrew. Yitzhak Ben-Ner's long, rather melodramatic *Protocol* (1983), a novel about a cell of Jewish communists in Palestine of the 1920s, is written in the Hebrew of that period, which, roughly, is about as far from current usage as eighteenth-century English from contemporary English. Adopting period language is of course a familiar strategy for producing an effect of authenticity in a historical novel, but in this book about political factionalism and fanaticism within the Zionist community, there is a particular sense of how language mirrors ideology – all the more sharply in the case of a language that in a sense is being reinvented from day to day not only to serve practical purposes but also to express a set of ideological values.

The ideological valence of language is felt in another way when different strata of Hebrew are juxtaposed in the same work as a kind of historical heteroglossia. In David Grossman's *See Under: Love* (1986), the concentration camp survivor, Anshel Wasserman, speaks throughout in the quaint Haskalah Hebrew in which he wrote his juvenile fiction early in the century. For the Hebrew reader, I would say, this device, despite the grim subject of the novel, produces a vaguely amusing effect, but it also has serious thematic implications. Anshel's language, studded with scriptural allusions and rabbinic locutions, redolent of that infatuation with the Hebrew medium which is one of the hallmarks of the Haskalah, reflects the innocent faith of the old European Hebraism in language as such, the Hebrew language in particular, and the prospect of a renewed Hebrew culture that would take its natural place in the brotherhood of enlightened modern cultures. (Ironically, if improbably, Anshel's books have been translated into German and once fed the imagination of the novel's death camp commandant in his idealistic boyhood.) Anshel finds himself in historical circumstances that make the cruelest mockery of such innocent faith in the enlightening efficacy of literary language, and Grossman's deployment of different Hebrew dictions interrogates the adequacy of any use of language – colloquial, poetic, scientific, as well as Anshel's quaintly mannered old-fashioned Hebrew – to respond to the horror of recent history.

The most spectacular instance of linguistic archeology in recent Israeli fiction is A. B. Yehoshua's *Mr. Mani* (1990), a novel structured as five long "conversations" that move in reverse chronological order from 1982 to 1848. Only the first of the five speakers is presumed in the fictional setting actually to be speaking Hebrew, and her language is contemporary colloquial. The second and third conversations, supposed to take place respectively in German and English, are a little problematic because it is not clear that Yehoshua's Hebrew is entirely persuasive in recreating the social and cultural registers of the two foreign speakers, a German soldier in World War II and an Anglo-Jewish junior officer in World War I. It is perhaps not coincidental that the two most compelling chapters, the fourth and the fifth, are the ones that in different ways highlight Hebrew as a battleground of modern Jewish ideologies. The fourth conversation takes place in Poland a few months after the Third Zionist Congress in 1899 and is presumed to be in Yiddish. Terms borrowed from turn-of-the-century Hebrew fiction in Eastern Europe give the conversation an appropriate period flavor, which then becomes a linguistic counterpoint to the enigmatically Sephardic Mr. Mani at the center of the speaker's story and to the flaunted Sephardicness of the final chapter. This last conversation would actually be in Ladino, but given the pious world of the speaker and his two interlocutors, Yehoshua is able to create a highly plausible equivalent for the Sephardic vernacular through a richly traditional Hebrew woven from the language of sacred texts. The novel as a whole is a fascinating attempt to reimagine Zionism, the relations between Arab and Jew as well as between Ashkenazi and Sephardi, the Mediterranean dimension of Jewish identity, and the correspondence of all these with the convolutions of psychosexual life, conscious and unconscious. I don't want to reduce it merely to a problematic of language. But Yehoshua's excavative descent through strata of Hebrew (which of course is not easy to see in translation) does focus attention on the complex intertwining of language, culture, and ideology. When one reaches the pungent premodern Hebrew of the last conversation, one sees in a single linguistic tapestry strands that anticipate Zionist consciousness, strands that express a national or messianic awareness other than political, strands that lead back to the cultural, commercial, and vividly sensual involvement of the Jews in the Mediterranean world. The Hebrew language, this book reminds us, is still an instrument for the shaping, the sustaining, and perhaps in some ways also for the distorting of Jewish national identity.

Nothing I have said compromises the obvious truth that literature written in Hebrew is amenable to the same empirical principles of comparative literary history and descriptive poetics as any of the literatures more familiar to Western readers. Uri Zvi Greenberg (1896–1983) produced a body of powerful poetry that can be usefully analyzed in terms of its relation to the ferment of European avant-garde movements that affected him in his youth and to German Expressionism in particular. Formally, his free-verse rhythms and expansive lines as well as his cultivation of a bardic poetic persona owe a good deal to the model of Walt Whitman, whose name Greenberg invokes in his early poetic manifestoes. A formalist critic, a literary historian, a theorist of poetic modernism could all appropriately speak of Greenberg in more or less the same terms they might use for, say, Alexsandr Blok. At the same time, however, one can scarcely ignore Greenberg's consciousness of Hebrew as a contested language with a unique pedigree (implicitly manifested in his own move from an initial phase in Yiddish to Hebrew). And one is constantly struck by the powerful echo chamber effect of Greenberg's Hebrew, playing on resonances from the language of the Bible, the Talmud and Midrash, the liturgy, and the Hasidic masters. Moreover, no other Hebrew poet has generated ideological ardor through his language with Greenberg's daunting intensity, insisting in the imaginative momentum of his particular Hebrew lexicon on apocalyptic, militant, racist, even monarchist perspectives for seeing contemporary events. There is no stronger literary instance of Scholem's notion about how the revival of the language conjures up the dangerous potencies of old Hebrew words.

These persistent anomalies of modern Hebrew literature, for which Greenberg could serve as a textbook example, are tokens of the residual but stubborn resistance of the Jewish people to that purportedly salutary process of normalization which was one of the goals of the Zionist movement. One could argue that the founding fathers of modern Hebrew literature in Enlightenment Germany were already looking to their own horizon of normalization, though they did not use the term. They and their heirs all the way down to new Israeli writers like David Grossman, Meir Shalev, and Yehudit Katzir, have abundantly succeeded in making Hebrew a literature like other literatures, and at least as lively and various as any other. Yet the circumstances of Jewish historical experience have been so odd, so paradoxical and multilayered, that the literature continues to bear traces of its peculiar cultural origins. Indeed, it remains the most acutely sensitive barometer for the perennially turbulent inner atmospheres of the people to which it is addressed.

2

SECULARITY AND

THE TRADITION OF

HEBREW VERSE

Once every few decades, an anthology appears that reaches beyond mere scissors-and-paste operations to restore to contemporary readers a lost literary past. A notable instance in English was the publication exactly sixty years ago of H. J. C. Grierson's *Metaphysical Lyrics and Poems*, which, coming at the very moment when T. S. Eliot and others were rebelling against the norms of nineteenth-century verse, brought back into the main line of the English tradition the passionately witty poets of the seventeenth century like Donne, Herbert, and Marvell who had long been discredited, misunderstood, or even half-forgotten.

The publication of T. Carmi's *The Penguin Book of Hebrew Verse* is such an event of recuperation, not only for English readers but for readers of Hebrew as well, who will discover in this bilingual volume unguessed treasures, a few of them appearing in print for the first time, others never before published out of their original liturgical contexts, or, in the case of the secular poems, many never anthologized or published in modern critical editions. There has been, in fact, as Carmi justly observes in his preface, no anthology like this in Hebrew that covers the full three-thousand-year span of Hebrew poetry. Though the earliest part of Carmi's anthology, a selection of fourteen biblical poems from the victory hymn in Exodus 15 to the Song of Songs, may be superfluous for some readers, it does lay the ground for one of the important revelations of the volume: the astonishing degree of continuity exhibited by Hebrew poetry through its long history and its wide geographical dispersal.

It was, of course, chiefly the authority of the Bible, both as linguistic standard and as a source of imagery and allusions, that preserved this continuity through so many different eras and cultural spheres. The *piyyut*, or liturgical verse, of Palestine and Babylonia (roughly, sixth to eleventh centuries C.E.) is a partial exception to the rule of continuity because this particular tradition took disconcerting liberties with classical Hebrew grammar and vocabulary, and developed its own sometimes cryptic conventions of kenning and elaborate allusion. Elsewhere, however, the kinship of different Hebrew poems separated by centuries and continents is altogether remarkable. A reader of the poetry of Gabriel Preil and Yehuda Amichai written today, respectively, in New York and Jerusalem often scarcely has to shift linguistic or aesthetic gears to move into a poem composed in Renaissance Italy, Palestine under the Romans, or Babylonia in the sixth century B.C.E.

If *The Penguin Book of Hebrew Verse,* the product of more than a decade of painstaking research, rescues characteristic elements of a partly forgotten poetic past, it is, I would propose, even more important for what it reveals of the extraordinary variety of Jewish historical experience. Carmi has tried to make his selections historically representative, avoiding any obvious tilt toward modern preferences and concerns in his choice of the older texts. (He has also provided tactfully concise, helpful notes to the poems and a valuable introductory essay, to which is appended an incisive summary by Benjamin Hrushovski of the different systems of Hebrew versification.) In any case, from the end of the biblical period to the latter part of the tenth century, there is scarcely any secular Hebrew poetry that has come down to us, apart from a very occasional brief inset of satirical or eulogistic verse in the Talmud. And since liturgical poetry is manifestly the predominant poetic genre, at least quantitatively, through the entire medieval period, readers will find a good deal of it here, joined, after the onset of the Crusades, by a liberal sampling of dirges, some affecting and a few chiefly horrific, on the massacre of Jews.

These disparate Jewish communities over the ages were devout and, in some periods, acutely suffering communities, and the poems bear witness to both these aspects of the Jewish historical condition.

The invocation of devotion and suffering is inevitable, and yet those very terms entail a conjuring with stereotypes, while the vivid evidence of the poems themselves demonstrates the inadequacy of just such stereotypes of Jewish history. The Jews, so runs the formula, have always been a religion, or, according to a different ideological perspective, a religious civilization. The modern age, then, brings with it secularization, which makes troubling "inroads" on Jewish life. There is an obvious element of truth in this familiar way of conceiving things, but one wonders how accurate such an account might be if it should prove that during much of the premodern period, the secular and the religious were intimately intertwined, or that, instead of being opposed categories, the religious was often a pliable framework within which the secular could be given quiet or at times even flamboyant expression. All this is not easy to sort out because the tenor and circumstances of Jewish life over the centuries have varied so widely. A few examples, however, from different times and places may at least suggest something of the inadequacy of the conventional categories.

Let me begin with an anonymous poem — it is actually the opening section of a longer poem in the form of an alphabetic acrostic — composed in Palestine under the Byzantine empire, sometime between the fourth and the early seventh centuries. It is a liturgical piece, intended for use in public worship as part of the prayer for dew recited during the Passover festival. One could hardly imagine a more clear-cut instance of a religious poem — verses actually framed to serve an institutional function. Here is how it reads in Carmi's translation:˙

* Carmi's versions throughout are admirably fluent and precise. But following the pattern of the Penguin anthologies of foreign poetry, they are prose translations meant in the first instance to provide guidance to readers who can make out at least something of the original, and they do not pretend to suggest anything of the form or rhythm of the poems. Because my quotations here do not have the advantage of appearing, as does the English in the anthology itself, in columns of print parallel to the Hebrew, I have taken the liberty of arranging Carmi's prose versions in lines of verse, to give some faint indication of the shape of the poems.

I shall sing praises now that the time of the singing bird has come,
and I shall answer in song:
go in peace, rain.
I shall look at the deeds of my God, so pleasant in their season,
and sweetly say:
come in peace, dew.
The rains are over and gone, the winter is past;
everything is created with beauty;
go in peace, rain.
The mandrakes give forth their perfume in the lovers' garden;
sorrows are past:
come in peace, dew.
The earth is crowned with new grain and wine,
and everything cries:
go in peace, rain!

This gives a fair sense of the lovely lyric simplicity of the original, though, as one might guess, the Hebrew has a quality of delicate musicality absent from the English version (there is, to cite a single instance, a nicely orchestrated play of sound and meaning in "mandrakes," *dud'aim*, "lovers," *dodim*, and "sorrows," *dev'aim*). In regard to function, this is of course a liturgical poem and thus inevitably a religious one, but precisely what kind of experience is expressed in these lines? The poet naturally invokes God, Whose "deeds" in bringing about the change of the seasons are "so pleasant," but his accent falls decisively on the pleasantness of the created world. Indeed, in the first line of the Hebrew, he does not sing praises, which might suggest an explicit turning to God at the very beginning, but rather he utters song (*zemirot*), which aligns him more directly with the singing bird or nightingale (*zamir*) and places him in the great vernal chorus of nature. The poet responds to the sudden freshening of life and beauty in nature with an alertness of the senses that does not seem very different from, say, the famous opening lines of *The Canterbury Tales*, in which Chaucer celebrates the sweet showers of April and the movement of renewal they bring. I would not be so crass as to argue that what we have in these fifteen Hebrew lines is a secular poem in religious guise, but the poem does register a sense of the beauty of nature, including the elation of awakening physical desire, which one might say was not strictly required by the liturgical occasion.

There is, however, a further complication in the link between the status of these lines as liturgical poetry and as nature poetry. The central verses of the passage are virtually a pastiche of phrases from the Song of Songs. Now, the Song of Songs is read in synagogues on the Sabbath of Passover and so there is a kind of association of liturgical occasions here, but I don't think that entirely explains the presence of the biblical material in the poem. Whatever its allegorical interpretations, the Song of Songs was – and has continued to be for the millennium-and-a-half since the composition of this liturgical poem – the great luminous model for Hebrew love poetry and Hebrew poetry about spring. The images from the Song of Songs work here like those crumbs of Japanese paper Proust describes which, when immersed in water, magically stretch and take shape and color as flowers and people. The term pastiche I used a moment ago is a little misleading in its suggestion of inertness or mechanical activity, for what actually happens is that the biblical text springs to life again in the quickening medium of the poet's imagination, or to view the process from another angle, the Song of Songs serves as a powerful catalyst for the poet's imagination as he responds to the natural world around him. This is not in itself secular poetry, but it gives us a glimpse of the cultural matrix upon which, a few centuries later, an extraordinary tradition of Hebrew secular poetry would grow.

The Penguin Book of Hebrew Verse includes several other spring liturgy poems from different periods that, like the text we have just considered, stand on the threshold of becoming celebratory nature poems. Another kind of ritual occasion, the marriage ceremony, provides the pious framework for a variety of love poems: after secular verse had taken root in Spain, some of these epithalamia would be frankly erotic and, in the subsequent Italian period, even bawdy. But in the liturgy proper, as Carmi's variegated selections tend to show, the poetic imagination addresses itself to a wide spectrum of topics, and for some of these the liturgical occasion seems less a justification than an excuse.

Let me offer one relatively unfamiliar example. Middle Eastern Jewry, beginning in the tenth century or perhaps a little earlier, developed a special commemoration of the death of Moses that was associated with the fall festival of Simhat Torah. Carmi includes several poetic laments composed for this rite. The most recent of these is a strophic poem, cast in the form of a dialogue between the weeping Jochebed and her son Moses, probably written in the fifteenth century, possibly by Samuel ben Moses Dayan of Aleppo. In the penultimate stanza, Jochebed takes final leave of her son:

> Go then in peace, O you who pitched my tent!
> Your parting is a bitter thing for me, more bitter than any illness.
> May the Lord bestow His peace upon you and also upon me.
> May he listen to my bitter lament,
> and show His favor for your sake and for mine.

In a certain sense, this is more obviously a "religious" poem than the early Palestinian prayer for dew with its evocation of blossoming mandrakes and lovers' gardens. The subject, after all, is no less than the lawgiver of Israel, its liberator from Egyptian bondage, and the poem will actually conclude in the next stanza with a prayer for national redemption. One may nevertheless ask what these dramatized cries of a bereaved mother are doing in the liturgy for Simhat Torah. It goes without saying that the whole subject has no scriptural warrant, though the poet and his predecessors in this tradition had certain hints in the Midrash to draw from. The leading emphasis of the poem — perhaps in a sense its real subject — is neither Moses, the prophet of prophets, nor the redemption of Israel, but a mother's grief. The liturgical occasion and the biblical figures operate here in a manner roughly analogous to the iconography of the life of Jesus in Christian painting. That is, the iconography could be a vehicle for the devout representation of the central mystery of Christianity or it could serve as a means for the painter, using the traditional sacred figures, to explore visual and psychological themes of human existence like maternal beauty, childish innocence, suffering, compassion, bereavement. The various poems on the death of Moses, with their characteristic focus on the anguished mother, in fact look very much like a

Jewish pietà convention, though not in any way inspired by Christianity, since it evolved in the Islamic sphere.

Such intermittent pulsations of secular or perhaps rather humanistic feeling in the midst of devout expression may help explain the astounding alacrity exhibited by one major segment of medieval Jewry in adopting the secular high culture of the Arabs. This adoption, at least in the realm of literature, occurred almost overnight sometime in the latter part of the tenth century when a brash young man from Fez named Dunash ben Labrat arrived in Córdoba by way of Baghdad, where he had served as secretary to the illustrious rabbinic philosopher and legal authority, Saadia Gaon, and began to write secular poems in Hebrew after Arabic models, using the Arabic meters and rhyme schemes as well as the Arabic generic conventions. Many Jews were shocked by Dunash's innovations, and some pious objections to the new movement would persist for generations, but the greatest poetic talents of Andalusian Jewry very quickly followed his path.

Here on Iberian soil, the rickety opposition between secular and religious collapses in another way, for the Hebrew poets who wrote exquisite nature poems, richly sensual erotic verse, boisterous drinking songs, and mordant satire also produced sublime liturgical pieces — still following Arabic prosody — and personal religious poetry. The same figures who created such an exuberantly secular poetic corpus were also, variously, mystics, theologians, exegetes, and talmudic authorities. Thus, Solomon ibn Gabirol, the tortured mystic whose neoplatonic work, *Fons Vitae*, circulated in Latin translation for centuries among Christian religious thinkers, its Jewish authorship unknown, evokes an Andalusian garden at the beginning of the spring:

> With the ink of its showers and rains,
> with the quill of its lightning, with the hand of its clouds, winter
> wrote a letter upon the garden, in purple and blue.
> No artist could ever conceive the like of that.
> And this is why the earth, grown jealous of the sky,
> embroidered stars in the folds of the flowerbeds.

Or Judah Halevi, author of *The Kuzari,* the great medieval apologia for the Jewish faith, and also the supreme virtuoso of the Spanish Hebrew school, writes in a long lover's complaint to a coy mistress:

> Oh, after my death, let me still hear
> the sound of the golden bells on the hem of your skirt.
> And if you then ask how your beloved is, I, from the grave,
> will send you my love and my blessings!

And Abraham ibn Ezra, the famous biblical exegete and philologist who, arriving in Italy from his native Spain in the twelfth century, single-handedly Arabized its Hebrew poetics, as Dunash had done before him in Andalusia, writes of his own itinerant poverty with wry humor and candor:

> I have a cloak that is like a sieve
> to sift wheat or barley.
> I spread it out like a tent in the dark of night,
> and the stars shine through it;
> through it I see the moon and the Pleiades,
> and Orion flashing its light. . . .
> If a fly landed on it with its full weight,
> it would quickly regret its foolishness. . . .

The imaginative richness and variety of secular Hebrew poetry in Spain are familiar topics of celebration in the standard accounts of Jewish history. According to the most common notion, however, what occurred was a sudden sunburst of creativity in the eleventh and twelfth centuries—the period of the four commanding poets, Samuel Hanagid, Solomon ibn Gabirol, Moses ibn Ezra, and Judah Halevi—followed by a few after-glimmerings, then a general return to the norms of devotional ascesis and pious learning that prevailed in Jewish life until the seismic disruptions of modernity began to be felt in the eighteenth century. This view has remained entrenched because it allows one to think of the Hebrew Golden Age of Spain as an exception proving the comfortable stereotypical rule that defines premodern Jewry as a people of martyrs, scholars, and saints whose existence is everywhere pervaded by religiosity.

The untenability of such a view has been made evident by the re-

cent scholarly work in Hebrew of Dan Pagis on the manifold contin-
uations of the Hebrew secular tradition after the Spanish period.
Carmi, who gratefully acknowledges his debt to Pagis's researches, includes some impressive instances in his anthology of the lively persistence of secular verse well after the twelfth century. Geographically,
the movement that started in Andalusia spread to Christian Spain,
Provence, Italy, North Africa, Greece, and Turkey, as far east as Yemen,
as far north as Amsterdam. Chronologically, it constituted an unbroken tradition that ran on to the eighteenth century, where it over-
lapped with the Hebrew Enlightenment, which began in Germany as a
much more self-conscious and ideological movement of secularization emulating Central European literary models. The poems and novels that roll off the presses in Tel Aviv today are not merely the consequence of the Zionist revival over the past half-century or more but
are part of a thousand years of continuous secular literary activity in
Hebrew—fully half the period since the destruction of the Second
Temple.

It is, of course, important to keep in mind that Jews were doing
much besides writing amorous and satiric verse during this second
millennium of Diaspora existence. The flourishing of Hebrew poetry
in Spain was almost contemporaneous with the development of *Ha-
sidut Ashkenaz*, the mystical and ascetic pietistic movement that began in twelfth-century Germany, and with the emergence of the Kabbalah in Spain itself. In the centuries that followed, Jewish cultural
energies were characteristically expressed in exegesis of both the Bible
and the Talmud, in codes of law and in responsa, in devotional and
mystical treatises, in movements like the Hasidism of Eastern Europe
and the ascetic ethical regimen of *Musar* promulgated in many of the
great East European talmudic academies.

All this pious activity can hardly be thought of as peripheral. From
the thirteenth century on, the major thrust of Jewish imagination, its
real profundity and originality, indisputably moved through these various religious channels; and even in the classic age of Spain in the
eleventh and twelfth centuries, there were achievements in religious
philosophy and mystical writing as forcefully imaginative as the great

secular poems of the period and more comprehensive in scope. The best of this secular poetry in the Andalusian era is, I believe, on a par with the finest lyric poetry of the Western tradition, while Hebrew verse from the thirteenth to the eighteenth centuries, however lively and engaging, hardly has the same imaginative authority.

In any case, the abundance and vitality of secular literary activity in this period are historical facts to be reckoned with, and I suspect that prevailing ideas about the last several centuries of Jewish history would look rather different if they were not so centered in Ashkenazic Jewry. Jews in Central and Eastern Europe, especially in the last few centuries before modernity, lived by and large in enclaves, speaking their own language, not entirely sealed off from their Gentile surroundings but separated from them, one might say, by a semipermeable membrane. In contrast, the Sephardic Jews of Spain and Italy, though by no means free of legal discrimination and the threat of persecution or even physical violence, lived in much freer interaction with their host cultures. The eight-hundred-year tradition of Hebrew literature they created bears witness above all to the positive genius for assimilation that has been one of the central mechanisms of Jewish existence through the ages.

This genius for assimilation, to invoke a famous distinction of the Hebrew essayist, Ahad Ha'am, was a matter of competitive rather than self-effacing imitation. The Hebrew of the Bible, Dunash and his followers argued, was an even more perfect instrument of literary expression than the Arabic of the Koran, and anything they could do, we could do better—which the great Hebrew poets after Dunash proceeded to accomplish, fashioning the most brilliant and at times luxuriant poems according to all the Arabic topical conventions, using the same kind of imagery as the Arabic, but in an elaborately wrought indigenous Hebrew drawing on two millennia of Jewish tradition. The Hebrew writers absorbed from their Arabic models not only forms and conventions but also—for these are never wholly separable—a certain sensibility, a certain way of seeing the world, an inclination to cultivate or even revel in certain kinds of experience. If the writing of love poems, both heterosexual and (in accordance with Arabic convention) homosexual, was generally a literary exercise rather than a confession of personal involvement, it nevertheless entailed an imaginative immersion in the experience expressed, so that "mere" exercise often shades into personal expression, the latter becoming unambiguous in the case of a poet like Todros Abulafia of thirteenth-century Toledo, who describes some of his actual mistresses in verse and wittily defends his weakness for Arab and Christian girls.

The same process of assimilation occurred again in Italy. It is an instructive curiosity of literary history that the first language after Italian in which sonnets were written was not French or Spanish or English but Hebrew — by Immanuel of Rome, who was composing sonnets before the end of the thirteenth century, within decades after the form was invented. The Hebrew poets of Italy wrote ottava rima, terza rima, sestinas, whatever seemed elegant or challenging or merely fashionable in Italian poetic practice; and beyond such matters of form, they absorbed the imaginative cast of the *dolce stil nuovo*, of ribald comedy, of the Italian baroque and neoclassical movements. Some of these poets, beginning with Immanuel, also wrote in Italian, or on occasion composed ingenious bilingual poems, but the continuing appeal for them of writing in Hebrew, which of course was not a spoken language, as an expression of their cultural identity as Jews, is remarkable.

At times their language could be quite mannered, but often one is struck by its vivid immediacy, its capacity to sound *as though* it were the actual vernacular of the poet. Thus Jacob Frances, in a poem written in Leghorn on the occasion of his brother's marriage in 1656, begins: "Leave off, you poetasters, leave off your singing! / All your pens should be dragged along and flung on a dung heap! / Pooh, pooh to you, pooh and a thousand poohs!" It is a little hard to believe that the third line, *pu, pu aleikhem, pu v'elef pu,* could have been written before the revival of Hebrew as a spoken language, but it shows how far the Hebrew poets were moved in their emulation of vernacular models to give their language the pungency and suppleness of a living tongue.

The involvement of Jews in secular poetry is of course part of a broader pattern of involvement in secular cultural activities. Over this eight-century span from Spain to Italy, Jews were often at the forefront of medicine, mathematics, astronomy, and diplomatic service. More popularly, individual Jews were dancing masters (one of the earliest Italian treatises on dance was written in Hebrew), musicians, and actors, not to speak of gamblers, con men, or simple thieves. Leone Modena, who is represented in *The Penguin Book of Hebrew Verse* by a single penitential poem for Yom Kippur, encapsulates in his own life this multifaceted involvement of Italian Jewry in general culture, high and low. Carmi's biographical note for Modena is as wonderful as any of the poems themselves in the anthology:

> Judah Aryeh [Leone] Modena (1571–1648) was born in Venice and studied under the poet-grammarian Samuel Archevolti in Padua. A child prodigy, he translated passages from Ariosto's *Orlando Furioso* at the age of twelve. He became famous as a rabbi and preacher in Venice and was the author of the first autobiography in Hebrew, *The Life of Judah*. In this unusually revealing narrative he lists twenty-six professions at which he tried his hand, among them: *maestro di cappella*, author of an Italian comedy, *dayan* [rabbinical judge], alchemist (his son died of lead poisoning after one of the experiments), writer of amulets and talismans, and matchmaker. He was addicted to gambling and, as a result, was perpetually on the verge of penury. At the request of the English Ambassador in Venice, he wrote *Historia de riti ebraici* for presentation to King James I. An avid polemicist, he wrote famous tracts against Christianity, Karaism, and the Kabbalah, and a condemnation of games of chance.

The astronomic distance between popular preconceptions and this real life of a sixteenth-century Venetian Jew is vividly illustrated by Jonathan Miller's appalling television production of *The Merchant of Venice*, recently shown in America on the PBS network. As many viewers objected, Miller and his leading man, Warren Mitchell (*né* Maisel), compounded the hostility of Shakespeare's characterization by divesting Shylock of whatever elements of dignity the playwright had given him, presenting the rapacious merchant with the Yiddish accent and the immigrant tics of a Jew in an antisemitic anecdote.

What is especially revealing is that Miller and Mitchell, in a televised conversation about their production, could say with a sense of complacent authority as Jews that Shakespeare had perfectly caught the historical character of Jewish culture in stressing Shylock's puritanical recoil from life and its pleasures, and that their own version brought to the fore the sympathy for the Jew which they perceived in the text of the play. Their self-deception on this last point is not so puzzling as it might first seem, for the antisemitic stereotype is in several respects only the reverse side of the modern sentimental stereotype of a traditional Jew. In both these perspectives, a Jew of Venice or Amsterdam or Barcelona would be imagined in the same terms facilely attributed to the Jew of Vilna or Bialystok: a dour, slightly stooped, wan figure, preferably with beard untrimmed, enveloped in a drab, shapeless caftan, exhibiting a certain tendency to draw back into the shadows at the sound of Gentile footsteps, his deep-set eyes, however, gleaming with a strangely intense light—for the antisemite, the glow of avarice; for the sentimentalist, the luminous vision of mystical realms beyond the shards and fragments of a world in exile. In contrast to Leone Modena's twenty-six professions, sacred and profane, this stereotypical Jew is allowed only the most limited occupational repertoire: for the antisemite, he is of course a money lender, if not some more sinister conspirator against the property and life of innocent Christians; for the nostalgic philosemite, he is a rabbi, a sage, or perhaps a saintly beggar.

The opposition between the highly variegated facts of history and just this sort of stereotype is exposed in a peculiar way by a very different kind of anthology of Jewish poetry, *Voices within the Ark*, edited by Howard Schwartz and Anthony Rudolf. This bulky volume is subtitled "The Modern Jewish Poets," with an implicit emphasis on the definite article, for the editors, in a rage of inclusiveness, have tried to omit no one. Major figures like H. N. Bialik, Jacob Glatstein, and Paul Celan rub shoulders with poets who have never published a book of verse, and with some who did but might have done well not to. There are some fine poems here swimming among a sea of indifferent ones, but it is not easy for a reader to know how to navigate through this abundance of selections. To the editors' credit, they have begun with substantial sections of Hebrew and Yiddish poetry—nearly a third of the volume. There follows a long section of English-

language poets, almost half of the entire book, and the anthology concludes with a section devoted to "Other Languages" which, in
keeping with the aspirations to comprehensiveness, includes Am-
haric, Turkish, Slovene, and Serbo-Croatian.

Now, when for the purposes of such an anthology, you select material from Hebrew and Yiddish, you are free simply to choose the poems
you like best, for the Jewishness of the poetry is in a sense formally
underwritten by the indigenous Jewish character of the language: an
anthologist's selection of Yiddish or Hebrew verse need not be different in range or themes from a general anthology of French or German
verse. In the English and "Other Languages" sections, however, of
Voices within the Ark, the editors, naturally enough, felt a certain ob-
ligation to choose poems that reflected the particularly Jewish concerns of the poets. The result is an instructive documentation of the
constrained self-consciousness with which writers working outside a
comprehensive Jewish cultural context imagine Jewish experience
and strive to be Jewish.

There are a good many variations on explicitly biblical themes,
which has been a perennial form of Jewish expression in many languages, including Hebrew; also, predictably, there are frequent poetic
reflections on the mass murder of European Jewry. In the large middle
ground between ancient text and modern catastrophe, one encounters
a dense cluster of old rabbis, bearded Jews swaying in prayer shawls,
flickering Sabbath candles, wailing walls, open Talmud folios, Torah
scrolls, and angular Hebrew letters floating through the air or tangled
in burning bushes, à la Ben Shahn. One might well ponder the cultural
contrast between the modern Jewish poets in many languages mar-
shaling all these paraphernalia of sanctity and the Hebrew poets of
Spain, Italy, Greece, and Yemen in Carmi's anthology who write of
spring gardens, breasts that invite caresses, the pleasures of drinking,
the misery of old whores, the evils of patronage, the squalor of prison,
and the boisterousness of common inns, claiming as their natural
right of experience everything from humble cabbages to the grandeur
of kings.

Let me offer one last example from *The Penguin Book of Hebrew*

Verse as an illustration of the lively variety of premodern Jewish culture, the vigor with which a secular sensibility could flourish in the heart of an officially religious society, and through the means of the Holy Tongue. The poet in question is Immanuel Frances (1618-c.1710), the younger brother of Jacob Frances and his collaborator on many literary projects. Frances was not so extreme a conjunction of sacred and profane as Leone Modena, but like many Italian and Spanish Jews, he did some remarkable shuttling between the two. During the latter part of his long life, he served as a rabbi in Florence and was a respected authority on talmudic law. At the time of the Sabbatian upheaval of 1666, he was a trenchant opponent of the pseudomessiah and composed an anti-Sabbatian polemic in Hebrew with his brother. In all these regards, Immanuel Frances was certainly a pillar of the traditional community. He wrote liturgical poetry and also recitative religious works commissioned by musical societies. He also wrote Hebrew love poems after Italian generic models, and composed a treatise on poetics. Here is one of his love sonnets (in this one instance, I shall offer my own verse translation, reproducing the Petrarchan form of the original):

When Hannah I behold in shining light,
When I recall Naomi, passing fair —
My heart for Hannah leaps like flames in air,
Naomi makes my soul burn fire-bright.

Between two stools I fall in luckless plight:
Today it's Hannah's sovereignty I bear,
Before, Naomi was my constant care.
O, Love, where may I flee your searching sight?

Alas, as iron does on iron hone,
Desire upon desire whets its edge,
And so my thoughts from panic take their tone.

I beg you, Love, from fortune's narrow ledge:
O, grant me two hearts here instead of one,
Or split my heart in two with your swift wedge.

Although the language of this whole tradition of Hebrew poetry is often highly allusive, this particular sonnet is not much concerned with the echoes of classical Hebrew texts; what it does instead is to use the standard poetic vocabulary of amatory experience that goes back to tenth-century Spain in order to render in Hebrew a highly Italianate witty version of a lover's dilemma. There are just two readily identifiable allusions in the poem. One, in the first line of the sestet, would seem chiefly to be the idiomatic use of a well-known biblical image of strife ("As iron sharpens iron, so a man sharpens his fellow" [Prov. 27:17]), which is extended in the next line into a poetic conceit on the psychology of passion. The other allusion, in the last line of the octave, is to a famous expression of spiritual anguish ("Where may I escape Your spirit and where may I flee Your presence?" [Ps. 139:7]), and might conceivably be construed as blasphemous since God is replaced by omnipresent Love, to whom the poet will turn in prayer in the concluding tercet.

In regard to the larger historical reality reflected by such texts, what is most interesting is where to locate this poem in the experience of Immanuel Frances, rabbi, talmudist, and religious polemicist. It would obviously be naive to assume that the sonnet was literally autobiographical, that the good rabbi of Florence was really torn between an irreconcilable passion for a certain Hannah and a certain Naomi. (The names themselves look suspiciously like conventional literary devices, etymologically suggesting, respectively, grace and sweetness.) But I think it is almost as naive to assume, as some scholars have done, that poems like this are purely formal exercises with no experiential roots in the life of the poet. The act of creating poetry is hardly ever so exclusively cerebral. At the very least, the experience rendered in the poem was attractive enough to the poet for him to etch it in fourteen lines of carefully wrought verse, which means entering imaginatively into the fluctuations of fickleness and conflicting desire, and in the concluding conceit, the contemplation of a prospect of bigamous bliss contrary to the single-hearted condition of the human animal.

Was Immanuel Frances, rabbi of Florence, a pagan *à ses heures* when he, or at any rate a speaker he invented, turned to omnipresent Love in prayer? In a limited sense, yes, to the extent that he discovered in the literary convention of entreating the deity Love something attuned to what we undergo as human beings that was worth expressing, and that could not be expressed so sharply in strictly monotheistic terms. But the chief point about the sonnet, and about much of the body of Hebrew poetry with which it is linked, is that it is an act of playfulness.

Playfulness is not a quality much brought to mind in prevalent conceptions of premodern Jewry, featuring as they do an exalted but limited cast of mystic sages and tormented talmudists, but it is vibrantly evident in a major current of the last millennium of Jewish cultural history. Our modern tendency is to view Judaism as relentlessly imperative and generally problematic besides, but there is good evidence that many of our ancestors assumed it to be neither. Immanuel Frances was clearly not calling his faith into question in poetically imploring Love to help him solve his problems with Hannah and Naomi, but he may well have assumed that the context of faith was comprehensive yet not exactly pervasive, that one could be relaxed enough as a religious Jew to explore aesthetic and emotional experiences pleasurable in their own right which had nothing to do with precept and creed.

Such exploration does not make the poet a secularist but it is itself essentially secular. This recurrent élan of secular feeling in the midst of religious tradition, using the very language of tradition, is worth pondering. It suggests that Jewish experience before the modern era was more various, and even more paradoxical, than we are accustomed to think.

3

INVENTING

HEBREW PROSE

Most readers of fiction these days, in Israel and elsewhere, take for granted the viability of the Hebrew language as a vehicle of modern literary expression. Hebrew novels seem to get translated into English almost as fast as they are produced in the original; writers like Yaakov Shabtai, Aharon Appelfeld, Amos Oz, and A. B. Yehoshua have come to be seen as important figures on the international literary scene of the seventies and eighties; and the evidence of their prose—as well as that of still untranslated writers like Amalia Kahana-Carmon and Yitzhak Ben-Ner—clearly suggests that virtually all desired nuances of thought and feeling, virtually all the minute and peculiar details of external reality, can be caught in the supple meshes of the Hebrew language.

Behind these recent achievements, however, lies a long, uneven, and in some ways quite improbable growth of the language toward maturity as a medium of realistic fiction. When Hebrew literature emerged as a self-consciously modernizing movement in Central Europe more than two centuries ago, it was prose above all that was the technical problem for the new Hebraists. Hebrew, though not a spoken language, had been in continuous use as a literary language for three thousand years. To be sure, during certain periods, literary expression was confined to the religious spheres of liturgy and exegesis; but from the late tenth century C.E. onward there was an unbroken tradition of secular literature as well, stretching from medieval Andalusia to Renaissance and baroque Italy and Holland. The preponderant genre of this tradition was poetry, sometimes complemented by a wittily ornate form of rhymed narrative prose. More workmanlike varieties of prose served the purposes of philosophic discourse, manuals of devotion, chronicles, rabbinic responsa, travel books, and international business correspondence among Jews.

All this varied activity attests to the vitality of the language, to the fact that many Jews continued to regard it as their national tongue even though they did not speak it. But for the increasing number of writers who tried to create prose fiction in Hebrew through the middle and late decades of the nineteenth century, this hodgepodge of antecedents offered only partial and inadequate solutions to the problems of style, syntax, diction, and vocabulary with which they struggled. They aspired, after all, to achieve in Hebrew what Gogol and Turgenev had achieved in Russian, Balzac in French, Scott and Dickens in English; and how was one to do this in a language nobody spoke, in which it was difficult to discriminate levels of diction and even semantic borders between related terms, in which there was no word for "potato," and "gloves" could be indicated only by the awkward new coinage, "hand-houses"?

Altogether, the story of modern Hebrew literature in Europe is both intriguing in itself and generally instructive about the nature of the language of realism in literature; but, given the paucity of translations of these early modern Hebrew texts and of critical studies in Western languages, it is a story scarcely known outside the circle of readers of Hebrew. This is hardly the place to undertake a concise history of modern Hebrew literature, but it will be helpful to establish some general notion of where this literature came from and what were the circumstances under which, against all odds, it came to flourish.

The newness of modern Hebrew literature has long been a subject of debate among Hebrew literary historians because the supposed emergence of the modern movement in eighteenth-century Germany was preceded by that eight-centuries-long tradition of secular belletristic writing in Hebrew to which I have alluded. But the new movement that surfaced in Enlightenment Germany was, I think, different in kind from its predecessor because of its fundamentally ideological character. That is to say, by the late eighteenth century, European Jewry was launching the process of radical historical transformation we call modernization, and what was at issue now in the act of writing Hebrew was not just an aesthetic pursuit but a programmatic renegotiation of the terms of Jewish collective identity. It is surely not a coincidence that Christian Wilhelm von Dohm brought out his essay, "Concerning the Amelioration of the Civil Status of the Jews," in 1781, that Joseph II of Austria issued his Edict of Toleration in 1782, and that the founding journal of the Haskalah, or Hebrew Enlightenment, the quarterly *HaMe'asef*, began publication in Königsberg in 1783.

The Haskalah as a coherent movement would last a full century, until the trauma of the pogroms of 1881 made its rationalist meliorism untenable for most Hebrew writers, who then turned to nationalist and neo-Romantic literary trends. In its first decades, didactic essays and almost equally didactic poetry predominate, the writers being preoccupied with how to reform Jewish education, Jewish communal politics, Jewish social conditions, Jewish theology. The first instances of prose fiction, which begin to appear around 1820, are lampoons of Hasidic obscurantism and so partake of the general reformist impulse.

By this time, the Hebrew movement had moved eastward from its original centers in Berlin and Königsberg to Vienna, as the rapid progress of assimilation in Prussia eroded the base of Hebrew readers there. Though Vienna itself may be a "Central" European city, down to World War I its Jewish hinterland, we should remember, was Polish Galicia, also part of the Austro-Hungarian empire. Here and elsewhere, Hebrew literature was associated with the great Jewish migration from the small towns, or *shtetlakh*, to the cities that continued through much of the nineteenth century on into the early decades of the twentieth century. (One might recall, as notable instances of the general trend, that Jakob Freud and Hermann Kafka migrated from their native Galician *shtetlakh* to Vienna and Prague respectively, thus making possible the future careers of their illustrious sons.) Soon, there were centers of Haskalah activity in Galicia itself, in

Brody, Tarnopol, Lemberg, and Cracow; and by 1840 the new Hebrew literature had also put down roots in Lithuania and in Russia proper, where it was destined to attain its greatest achievements.

As I have noted, prose fiction was long a peripheral genre in the Haskalah: the first Hebrew novel does not appear until 1853, and an artistically mature body of fiction, free of didactic insistence and stylistically adequate to its subjects, does not begin to emerge until the 1880s. The eventual embracing of the novel form may well be another manifestation of the substantive newness of modern Hebrew literature in comparison with earlier phases of secular literature in Hebrew. The novel's generic project of comprehensive realism, of making language effect a kind of sovereign illusion of reality, set it off from earlier genres. To write, let us say, a sonnet or a poetic epigram in Hebrew was an act of competitive cultural imitation, but one carried out within the confines of a highly conventionalized formal structure, and as such chiefly an aesthetic exercise, however deep the feeling behind some of the individual poems. To write a novel in Hebrew, on the other hand, was to constitute a whole world in a language not actually spoken in the real-life equivalent of that world, yet treated by the writer as though it were really spoken, as though a persuasive illusion of reality could be conveyed through a purely literary language. It was, as I shall try to explain, to enter deeply into the mind-set of European culture with a thoroughness not characteristic of premodern Hebrew literature; it was to invent a new secular Hebrew cultural identity as though it were somehow, uncannily, native to the European sphere.

Who were the people who created this new literature? How did they get a knowledge of the language sufficient to such an undertaking? What were the material conditions in which a literature so anomalous sustained itself? The makers of modern Hebrew literature were, almost without exception, male and the products of an Orthodox upbringing. (In the earlier Haskalah, a good many still preserved some form of enlightened Orthodoxy; later on, the overwhelming majority of the writers were men who had broken decisively with the world of Jewish observance of their childhood.) The gender and the religious background of the writers were determined by the peculiar educational system developed by European Jewry before its entry into modernity; the system, in turn, was associated with the equally peculiar social structure of East European Jewry; and both require a little explanation.

One of the oddest — and most crucial — cultural circumstances of traditional East European Jewry was that its masses, by and large, lived under the conditions of an impoverished peasantry while enjoying almost universal literacy. They were not, of course, a peasantry in being able to work the land: for the most part, they eked out their living as middlemen, petty tradesmen (and often tradeswomen), peddlers, estate managers and tax collectors, publicans, artisans. But a typical *shtetl* house, as one can see from photographs and films taken in Poland as late as the 1920s, would have looked not very different from the makeshift quarters of a black sharecropper in the American South: a one-room shack with dirt floor, without plumbing, crowded by a family with many children, perhaps even with the addition of an old grandparent. One readily understands why Mendele Mokher Seforim, the greatest fictional chronicler of these Jews in the Russian Pale of Settlement, should call one of his typical towns Kabtsiel, or Beggarsville.

I have said that these near paupers and actual paupers were mostly literate, but it was a two-track literacy reflecting a two-track educational system. The girls were instructed at home to read the vernacular Yiddish, and since the Hebrew prayerbook was written in the same Hebrew alphabet as Yiddish, they could also, as grown women, in order to fulfill the impulse of piety, "read" the prayers as well, without however understanding more than isolated words and phrases. The boys began ḥeder, or elementary school, before the age of five, and were immersed in a curriculum that was entirely limited to the close study of Hebrew and, later, Aramaic texts.

The young boys were led through the Pentateuch verse by verse, each Hebrew phrase being given its Yiddish equivalent in a kind of oral interlinear translation. Other books of the Bible might be accorded some attention when preparation was being made for their public reading at the appointed festivals (Song of Songs at Passover, Ruth at Shavuot, and so forth), and biblical texts fixed in the daily prayers, including dozens of psalms, would be gotten by heart through sheer force of repeated recitation. But there would be no formal teaching of principles of grammar, no vocabulary lists, no exercises in composition. Indeed, the teenage students who happened to get hold of a Hebrew grammar treated it pretty much as underground literature, knowing that their rabbinical mentors would regard as an act of subversion any attempt to study the Holy Tongue systematically, with "secular" tools, as though it were a language just like any other.

By the time a boy reached the age of legal induction into Jewish manhood at thirteen, if he was an alert pupil and if his schoolmaster had not been totally incompetent (incompetence being more or less endemic to the system), he could read biblical Hebrew with an approximation of understanding, would have had some introduction to the primary rabbinic text, the Mishnah, and to the main medieval Hebrew commentaries on the Pentateuch, and would have a reasonably adequate understanding of the Hebrew of the prayerbook. In fact, the extreme unevenness of instruction meant that most products of the *ḥeder* were functionally illiterate in Hebrew, retaining only the most rudimentary vocabulary and a fuzzy or mangled understanding of particular texts.

After the age of thirteen, a large part of the student body dropped out, some after a year or more of additional instruction, to become apprentices, to assist in the family business, or otherwise to enter the workforce, and sometimes to be married off by their parents by the time they were fifteen. The more gifted went on to the yeshiva, or talmudic academy, often having to move to a larger town where there was such an institution. The subject of study at the yeshiva was exclusively the Babylonian Talmud, a vast corpus of texts composed in a mélange of Hebrew and its cognate language, Aramaic; as always, the language of discussion among students, and between students and teacher, was Yiddish.

The schooldays were long, the demands relentless; students worked over the difficult texts and their commentaries in pairs, and then listened to a general lesson from the yeshiva instructor. The complementary intellectual qualities they were encouraged to develop were a prodigious retention by heart of the talmudic texts and their biblical precedents (*beqi'ut*) and an analytic sharpness accompanied by ingenuity (*ḥarifut*). Most boys left the yeshiva by their late teens, some, having received ordination, to take up rabbinical posts, many, having entered into an arranged marriage, to enjoy a period of private learning subsidized by a prosperous father-in-law who was willing to pay this price in order to have his daughter married to a man of learning.

From the account I have offered, it must surely seem a mystery that anyone could have emerged from this educational system with a sufficient grasp of the Hebrew language to write an essay, a travel book, a sonnet, or, especially, a novel. The yeshiva population was the intellectual elite of Central and East European premodern Jewry. The Hebrew writers produced by the yeshivas were an elite within an elite. In part, I mean simply that they were the equivalent of the A+ students in the system, and certainly the evidence many of them offer of retentive memory and (to a lesser degree) of dialectic subtlety, of *beqi'ut* and *ḥarifut*, is formidable. But I am also referring to a rather special mental aptitude which was not necessarily given special value within the system but which would have abundant uses outside the system — something that the Germans call *Sprachgefühl*, an innate sense, like perfect pitch in music, for how language should properly sound, joined with a relish for the sonorities and the semantic colorations of Hebrew words in their classical idiomatic combinations.

Minds of this almost preternaturally prehensile cast would catch onto every nuanced collocation, every linguistic particle, in a traditional Hebrew text, both those that were part of the curriculum and those that were not. And as a new Hebrew culture began to shimmer before such unusual students as a radical alternative of Jewish identity to that of the Orthodox system, they would, even in the yeshiva milieu, do a good deal of reaching, often surreptitiously, beyond the curriculum — to the parts of the Bible not officially studied, to the medieval philosophers and poets, to those new-fangled Hebrew grammars, and, worst of all, to the godless journals, the poetry and fiction, of the new Hebrew literature.

Even a moderately receptive yeshiva student, who had stayed within the confines of the talmudic curriculum, would have been able by the age of eighteen to compose certain limited kinds of Hebrew texts – say, a florid prose letter to a future bride (to be translated to her) made up of a pastiche of biblical phrases, or an opinion on a question of talmudic law in a more businesslike rabbinic Hebrew with an admixture of Aramaic. But the elite of the elite, those prehensile minds I have described, having used the system against itself, would be able by the same age to produce in Hebrew a piece of popular science, a critical essay, a long poem in hexameters, a work of fiction. This was not a language anyone was speaking, certainly not in the nineteenth century, but out of a comprehensive familiarity with the large body of traditional Hebrew texts, biblical and postbiblical, and counting on an audience whose intimate acquaintance with this corpus matched their own, these young men could compose quite freely in Hebrew.

To compose well, making the language address modern predicaments persuasively, was another matter: and it will be worth the effort to try to understand how the trailblazers accomplished that task.

The class background of the Hebrew writers is elusive. It is sometimes said that they derived chiefly from the merchant class – Ezra Spicehandler, for example, suggests that in the early nineteenth century the great trade fair at Leipzig was a center of transmission of the German Haskalah to the east through the contacts there between merchants from Prussia and from Polish Galicia. But "merchant" may be a little misleading because in Jewish society it embraced everything from prosperous fur traders and timber dealers to people who maintained wretched little stands in the streets for the sale of odds and ends. The writers came as frequently from the bottom rungs as from the top of the mercantile hierarchy, and so they can scarcely be said to represent an economically privileged class. In a typical poor family, an adolescent son would be expected to help support the household by working full time. But this was, after all, a society that placed immense value on learning, and in which learning was a means of social ascent; so when a boy showed signs of intellectual gifts by the age of thirteen, great efforts would be made to enable him to continue his studies, poverty notwithstanding. Given the talmudic route to Hebrew literacy, no doubt reinforced by a certain genetic background of intellectual aptitude, it is not surprising that a good many of the Hebrew writers had fathers who were members of the rabbinic intelligentsia—yeshiva instructors or even yeshiva directors, local rabbis, ritual slaughterers (a function that required talmudic learning), and independent scholars of Jewish law.

The one social class drastically underrepresented among Hebrew writers was the new Jewish urban proletariat that had formed in the industrializing cities of Central and Eastern Europe by the latter part of the nineteenth century. Perhaps this is because this class was more rapidly removed from the sources of rabbinic learning than any other in Jewish society. In any case, when members of the Jewish proletariat thought about a programmatic renegotiation of the terms of collective existence, it was typically through socialism, and the language used was the language of the Jewish masses, Yiddish. Although it is true that Yiddish and Hebrew during this period were cognate literatures, and that many of the important writers produced work in both languages, it is only Yiddish that evinces a general association with the values and aspirations of the urban proletariat. A surprisingly small proportion of the Hebrew writers were born in the large cities. For the most part, they ended up in the cities, where they sought modern culture, freedom from the restrictions of Orthodox society, and a sustaining coterie of like-minded secularist Hebrew littérateurs. Their writing, however, often concentrated on their native *shtetl* world or, alternatively, on the deracination of the Jewish intellectual displaced from the *shtetl* and struggling to find himself in the anonymity of the modern city.

It is hard to imagine how these men, impelled by the quixotic vision of creating a new secular literature out of a sacred language, managed to sustain themselves, not to speak of how they managed to sustain their common enterprise. Serving as Hebrew tutors to the sons and daughters of affluent Jewish families in the cities was one characteristic means of meager support. Some earned a living as editors, correspondents, even typesetters in whatever existed in the way of Hebrew journalism (more of which in a moment). Although most of them were autodidacts, some managed to obtain university degrees, usually by migrating from Russia, where they were excluded by the *numerus clausus*, to Germany or Switzerland, and a few were able to practice one of the trained professions. By and large, the economic circumstances of Hebrew writers in Europe are an unbroken hard-luck story, and so their sheer persistence in their literary enterprise bears witness to their fierce commitment to the idea of creating a modern literature in Hebrew.

We do not have precise data on the numerical size of this movement, but it could never have been very large. As I have intimated, the chief defining focus of the Hebrew revival was the literary periodical, from eighteenth-century Königsberg to twentieth-century Odessa and Warsaw, and the circulation of most of these would not have exceeded that of a highly specialized American scholarly journal. The pioneer publication, *HaMe'asef*, probably had no more than a thousand or so subscribers at the outset; by the time it was faltering, in 1797, it had only 120 subscribers, and yet it managed to limp on, appearing sporadically, for another twenty-two years, still thought of in Haskalah circles to the east as an important source of ideas and literary models. The Hebrew journals were often quarterlies, sometimes monthlies; *HaYom*, the first Hebrew daily, was issued in Petersburg in 1886. Toward the end of the nineteenth century, *HaTsefirah*, for a while also published as a daily, sold in Russia as many as fifteen thousand copies per issue.

This was in all likelihood the outer limit for circulation of anything published in Hebrew. The typical journal would have had no more than a couple of thousand subscribers, and most volumes of fiction or poetry would have had printings of the same magnitude, occasionally a little larger, often even smaller. If we add to our calculation the probable circumstance that copies of journals and books would have been shared by several readers, it is still unlikely that most works published in Hebrew in the nineteenth and early twentieth centuries were actually read by more than ten thousand people.

Why, then, would anyone with literary ambitions choose to pursue them under such difficult conditions? And indeed, the writers were not free of moments of despair: a famous case in point is the poem "For Whom Do I Labor?" in which Y. L. Gordon, the major poet of the Russian Haskalah, imagines he is the last of the Hebrew bards as his audience disappears into the vistas of assimilation.

There was, to begin with, a negative reason for the fidelity to Hebrew: most of the writers taught themselves Russian, or German, or Polish in adolescence or after and did not have sufficient mastery of the language of the general culture to write in it. Yiddish, of course, always remained an alternative; but in the minds of many of the writers it was associated with a culture they sought to transcend, a culture that lacked prestige for them. To restate this attitude in positive terms, a whole set of values was associated with Hebrew, as the classical language of Jewish culture, that Yiddish, even when it was felt by writers to have the intimate appeal of a native language rich in colloquial nuance, could not offer.

Only Hebrew spanned more than three millennia of national experience and had been used by Jews in all the far-flung regions of the Diaspora. Only Hebrew was associated with Jewish political autonomy, and the awareness of this association played a crucial role in Hebrew literature long before, and beyond, the emergence of political Zionism. For if Jews were to create a culture like others, not dominated by a clerical establishment and not defined exclusively in religious terms, the great historical model had been cast in Hebrew on the soil of ancient Palestine. The biblical texts, moreover, in their sublime poetry and their brilliant narratives, had a cachet of literary prestige for which Yiddish could offer no equivalent.

Ultimately, it seems to me that the passionate commitment to Hebrew was impelled in shifting proportions by both aesthetic and historical-ideological motives. On the aesthetic side, Hebrew had always been the most valued language of Jewish culture, if not the most commonly used in everyday life, and had long been the medium of refined literary exercises and epistolary art. With a certain aestheticization of Jewish culture that was a symptom of modernity, this attitude toward the language became for some a kind of addiction to its beauties, even to its sheer formal properties: one relished a well-turned Hebrew phrase, an elegant Hebrew sentence, as elsewhere one might relish Mozart or Cimarosa. The abiding delights of this aesthetic addiction could not be replaced for these writers by any other language, not even by their native tongue.

At the same time, many of the writers had a compelling awareness that this language was not only beautiful but timeless—a consideration usually powerful enough to outweigh whatever anxiety they might have felt about the tininess of their audiences. As S. Y. Agnon, a writer closer to our time but deriving from this Central European milieu before World War I, once observed of his own classicizing style: "My language [is] a simple, easy language, the language of all the generations before us and of all the generations to come." Though few Hebrew writers would have stated matters so flatly, in such a provocatively false-naive manner, Agnon's assertion expresses a fundamental feeling about the historical role of the language that many shared.

In sum, the creators of modern Hebrew literature in Europe were impelled by a sense that the language through which they sought to shape a new Jewish culture had a unique aesthetic dignity and a unique historical resonance. This sense sustained them in the shabbiest material circumstances, when there was barely a readership to address, when the great culture to come was represented here and now only by the handful of literary colleagues with whom they fraternized and with whom they collaborated on the new Hebrew journals and in the new publishing houses.

But even the most ardent loyalty to the language as a repository of distinctive values could not conceal the awkwardness and the artificiality of classical Hebrew as a medium for the representation of modern realities, whether social, historical, relational, or psychological. What was needed to make Hebrew transcend these inadequacies was the bold intervention of genius, which would find ways to make the old language answer to a radically new world.

This shaping of an artistically viable realistic Hebrew prose was achieved in two stages. The first stage was effected from the 1880s onward by a single extraordinary writer who was rapidly followed by a whole school of stylistic disciples. The second stage emerged around the turn of the century as a vehement reaction against the first which nevertheless built upon it. In order to understand these developments, we need to trace the story of Hebrew prose back to the Haskalah proper.

Although the prose of the Haskalah was by no means consistently biblical, it evinced a pronounced biblicizing tendency, especially in fiction. This meant a renunciation of the other major historical stratum of the language, rabbinic Hebrew (the language of the Midrash, the Mishnah, and the Hebrew elements of the Gemara). Now, rabbinic Hebrew in fact has a much larger and more nuanced vocabulary and a more flexible and precise syntax than biblical Hebrew, but in the minds of the new Hebraists it was the language of the Bible that had the aura of cultural prestige, while rabbinic Hebrew was associated with the narrow learning of *shtetl* and ghetto which they aspired to transcend. Many writers of the Hebrew Enlightenment seem mesmerized by the intrinsic magic of the lofty biblical phrase (*melitsa*, which was also a synonym for poetry itself in their usage but would later come to mean something like "overblown rhetoric"). The prose that was produced out of this aesthetic conviction is often a lifeless pastiche of biblical fragments, and when it attempts contemporary subjects one usually feels a grotesque disparity between the organizing patterns and lexical scope of the prose and the mental and material world of the characters.

In 1862, a twenty-six-year-old writer named Shalom Yakov Abramowitz published a short novel called, in a phrase from Isaiah with a didactic flourish characteristic of the Haskalah, *Learn to Do Well*. Although the writing exhibited a virtuoso's mastery of classical Hebrew, it also suffered conspicuously from the faults of the pastiche style that I just noted. Six years later, he reissued the novel with substantial revisions, now giving it the Turgenevan title, *Fathers and Sons*, but not really solving its artistic problems, as he himself quickly recognized. For he now abandoned Hebrew altogether, and during the next eighteen years, writing in Yiddish a brilliant series of satirical novels about Jewish life in the Pale of Settlement through an invented narrative persona, Mendele Mokher Seforim, Mendele the Bookseller, he became the acknowledged "grandfather" of the Yiddish novel. When he returned to Hebrew composition in 1886, producing new stories and reworking his Yiddish novels into Hebrew, he had arrived at a point where he could give Hebrew much of the pungency, the liveliness, the suppleness of the Yiddish he had been writing.

The two chief stylistic moves that enabled Mendele to achieve this unlikely feat were a switch to rabbinic Hebrew and a radically new use of allusions to classical Hebrew texts. In fact, his compendious prose incorporated virtually all the historical strata of the language – biblical, rabbinic, liturgic, medieval-philosophic, devotional, Hasidic – but everything was contained within a normative framework of rabbinic idiom, grammar, and syntax. This general adherence to the language of the early rabbis produced a sense of stylistic homogeneity, despite the inclusion of heterogeneous elements. Even more important, rabbinic syntax with its abundant possibilities of subordination made available a new precision in the definition of causal relations, just as its system of verb tenses offered a new complexity in the representation of temporal relations. And from the rabbinic sources, teeming as they are with references to the minutiae of everyday experience, Mendele culled a rich vocabulary with which it became possible to offer vivid depictions of everything from a broken-down horse pulling a wagon and a beggar in rags to a man patiently filling his pipe, lighting it with a glowing coal held in tongs, puffing it up, and relaxing into the pleasure of a leisurely smoke.

At the same time, the profuse allusions to both biblical and post-biblical texts, intended of course for the delectation of an audience scarcely less learned than the writer himself, were transformed from inert fragments of a pastiche into satiric flashpoints, repeatedly illuminating the discrepancy, or the wryly ironic congruence, between classical model and the modern reality. An 1890 story, for example, called "Shem and Japheth on the Train," begins with a description of an unruly mob of ragtag Jews trying to conduct trade as they crowd into the third-class compartments. On the surface, the prose seems Dickensian or Gogolian, but it also reverberates with echoes from the Exodus story and the story of the Golden Calf, suggesting expulsion, without the dignity of liberation, as a recurrent historical fate of the Jewish people and proffering the fixation on gold as an immemorial national propensity.

The major Hebrew poet, H. N. Bialik, a self-avowed disciple of Mendele in his own prose style, nicely summarized the master's achievement by calling him, in an essay written in 1910, "the creator of the *nusakh*." A *nusakh* is a traditional musical mode for chanting prayers in public ,worship. Anyone with a musical ear can learn a *nusakh*; once you know it, you can intone any set of words from the service and so act as prayer leader. Its three most prominent features are transmissibility (Bialik stresses that the *nusakh* is a collective possession), adaptability to new circumstances (any text can be sung to it), and its status as clarified form, exhibiting a modal unity. In regard to the last of these three traits, it should be observed that Mendele's prose evinces not only a stylistic consistency in adhering to rabbinic norms but a fondness for symmetries and balance, a predisposition to arrange strings of overlapping or nearly synonymous terms in nicely ordered pairs and triplets (Bialik notes the "solidity" of Mendele's style).

There was a powerful allure in the traditionalism and the internal harmony of this prose: for an approximate English equivalent, one would have to go back to the eighteenth century, to Johnson or Fielding. Within a decade of Mendele's return to Hebrew, dozens of writers were turning out *nusakh* prose. The last, and most extravagant, practitioner of the *nusakh*, Haim Hazaz, died as recently as 1973, and the influence of the tradition has been so pervasive that one still encounters little turns of phrase that hark back to the *nusakh* in Hebrew journalism today and, perhaps more frequently, in a certain style of Israeli political rhetoric.

But by the beginning of the twentieth century, a number of young writers had come to feel that Mendele's stylistic synthesis was a solution that did not respond to the imperative of realism as they perceived it. There was, of course, a certain tonal fit between the Jews of the Pale who inhabited Mendele's stories and novels and the Hebrew in which they were represented, for at least the males among them were, after all, study-house Jews or Jews who had rubbed against the world of the *ḥeder* and study-house, however imperfect their actual learning. Their very ne'er-do-well woolgathering drew on the idiom of the rabbinic texts, so the Hebrew Mendele uses for them is, paradoxically, flesh of their flesh, bone of their spiritual bone, even as we remember that their real-life counterparts would in fact have been speaking and dreaming and counting in Yiddish. Many of the younger Hebrew writers, however, like M. Y. Berdichevsky, Y. H. Brenner, and U. N. Gnessin, were interested in representing deracinated Jewish intellectuals in urban settings, and for such figures the language of the *nusakh* belonged to a world of values and concerns which the characters had put behind them. And the writers were not content to refer to modern experience largely through the indirection of ironic allusion, in the manner of Mendele.

There were still more substantive problems with Mendele's prose. Its classicizing balance did not accord with the new writers' interest in representing what was discordant, fragmentary, contradictory, ambiguous, and confused in human relations and inner experience. In fact, Mendele offered a model of prose as splendidly wrought artifact, whereas the new writers were variously concerned instead with evoking *process* in their writing. And as an extension of this last contrast, the *nusakh* style provides a sharp external view of the characters but does not lend itself very readily to rendering the characters' inwardness, to techniques like *style indirect libre* and interior monologue. By the first decade of our century, many Hebrew writers, like their English, French, German, and Russian contemporaries, were above all drawn to the fluctuating movements of consciousness as the proper arena for the enactment of serious fiction.

How could Hebrew, still without a vernacular base, be made the medium for a realism that was experiential and not social, as it had been for Mendele? To begin with, it was necessary to write what a purist would no doubt regard as bad Hebrew. I say bad in order to emphasize the energy of opposition or avoidance in this new writing. The symmetries and harmonies of the *nusakh* had to be shattered in order to achieve a closer approach to the kinetic reality of consciousness. The elegance of perfectly attuned classical Hebrew idioms had to be abandoned and in many instances actually replaced by what amounted to a Hebrew translation of European idioms, for it was the latter that more faithfully represented the unvoiced inner speech of the Europeanized characters.

If one tries to think about the Western novel in generic overview, there are of course striking stylistic differences among writers as well as notable shifts from one generation of writers to the next, but there is also a kind of loose consensus of stylistic predilections – say, from Stendhal to Flaubert to Tolstoy to Conrad and Mann – which one might call, with a necessary tincture of ironic qualification, Standard Novelistic. This consensus would include the sense of narration, from larger units down to sentence structure, as slow cumulative process; a fondness for analytic discriminations and proliferating qualifications, for lists and the endlessly additive assemblage of details; and a flexible, constantly mobile use of narrative stance, shuttling back and forth among authorial commentary, report of scene and action, quoted monologue, third-person rendering of unspoken inner speech, summary of thought and feeling.

The anti-*nusakh* writers of the early 1900s, whether they had specific European models in mind or not (Dostoevsky, Chekhov, and lesser Russian and German writers were variously sources of partial inspiration), were essentially trying to make Hebrew work as a dialect of Standard Novelistic. With regard to the history of the Hebrew language, then, it is instructive to note that the process of Europeanization that many linguists have observed in Israeli Hebrew actually began in the composition of fiction a good quarter-century before Hebrew was fully revived as a spoken language. This revolutionary change at times results in grating effects, especially in the prose of Brenner and Berdichevsky, but the rapid success of the undertaking is quite remarkable.

A full demonstration of this success would require lengthy quotation and analysis, but let me offer just a small fragment of a sentence from Gnessin – he is a writer who tends toward paragraph-long sentences – as an illustration of the new orientation toward style in early Hebrew modernism. The protagonist of his 1906 novella *To the Side* is, like the central figure of many a modernist fiction elsewhere, a man without much vocation for living – neurasthenic, sexually insecure and self-subverting, dreaming of professional achievement and private consummation without the will to effect them. Here is the report of a characteristic moment in his chronic condition of quiet desperation:

> and the heart felt as though some thin crust were peeling off within it, and that thin crust were peeling and splitting and separating into bubbles, and these were sliding, sliding out and pressing against the chest and bursting into the throat.

The unpleasant but effective simile of the bursting crust and the sliding bubbles is not dictated by any conventional literary decorum or by a traditional association of idioms but rather by the desire to be faithful to the kinesthetic reality of the represented experience. The overlapping, additive movement of the syntax does not reflect any established rhetorical norm of sentence structure but rather the commitment to the verbal intimation of process of which I have spoken.

In precisely this regard, Gnessin actually shifts the center of gravity of the system of Hebrew verb tenses. Instead of simple past (Hebrew: *pa'al*) he repeatedly prefers either an iterative past or, as here, a progressive past (in Hebrew, both have the same form, *hayah po'el*). The effect is as momentous as that of the analogous shift Erich Auerbach observed long ago in Flaubert's French from *passé simple* to *imparfait*: instead of a world of clearly demarcated events following one another in steady sequence, things happen habitually, over and over, the units of time blurring together; or, alternately, there is a movement of minutely calibrated process in a kind of experiential slow motion, as in the figurative language here we edge through the progressive verbs from peeling to splitting to separating, sliding, pressing, and finally bursting.

Gnessin, who died of tuberculosis in 1913 at the age of thirty-two, leaving behind only a small handful of remarkable short fictions, achieved the most subtle and complex effects of any of the creators of modernist prose in Hebrew. It took more than half a century before Hebrew criticism began to appreciate the extent of his originality, though he had a few stylistic heirs in the next generation of Hebrew writers. One was Simon Halkin, who wrote in this country two densely lyric novels about American Jews before he emigrated to Israel in the late 1940s; another was David Fogel, like Halkin also a prominent poet, who produced some extraordinary fiction, thoroughly European in character, concerned with the psychological convolutions of erotic life, while he was living in Paris in the twenties and thirties. (He was to perish in a Nazi death camp.)

In addition to its stylistically iconoclastic impulse, the modernist movement in Hebrew exhibits through the early decades of the century the most impressive growth of precision in the nuanced use of terms. In part, this is a consequence of creating through repeated literary usage a consensus on the precise semantic range of classical Hebrew terms. But Mendele's mining of the lexical wealth offered by rabbinic and postrabbinic sources was also crucial for the very writers who rebelled against his model of indigenously Hebrew prose artifact. For these sources offered writers of fiction the vocabulary to describe the streaks of the lily, the beads of moisture on the grimy windowpane, the wart on the bulbous nose, and even the various modes of consciousness and inner states of being.

Thus, a single passage in a novella by David Fogel representing a woman's disturbed state of arousal in the presence of a sexually overpowering man uses *yeshut*, a medieval philosophic term that means in context "inward self"; *da'at*, "mind," a biblical and rabbinic term; *havayah*, "essential being," a rabbinic word originally meaning "that which is"; and soon after we encounter *hakarah*, "consciousness," a new acceptation, under the pressure of analogous European usages, for a rabbinic term that indicates recognition or knowing. Very little of this literary vocabulary, which has been inherited by contemporary Israeli writers, consists of loanwords, a fact that makes the acquisition of literary Hebrew to this day a difficult task for anyone who has not grown up with the language.

The precedent of the *nusakh* was important for the anti-*nusakh* writers in other ways as well. Although their own prose, for the reasons I have offered, no longer paraded ostentatiously in the bookish finery of rabbinic learning, juggling sources as it went, they followed Mendele in fixing rabbinic syntax and grammar as the prevailing norm, a formal decision which made possible the kind of suppleness of statement and complication of temporality and relation they sought. The model of rabbinic Hebrew, moreover, opened an avenue to vernacular vitality in a language nobody as yet spoke.

Mendele as a composer of Yiddish prose had exploited the vernacular vividness of the actual folk language. When he came back to Hebrew, still using a narrator who was a kind of oral performer, he needed to create some Hebrew equivalent for the liveliness of the spoken word. The rabbinic texts on which he now drew made a crucial difference in this regard because they are filled with living voices. The Mishnah is a written compilation of what was initially an oral study of the Law, and it retains in the very cadences and turns of speech of its questions and responses and conclusions abundant traces of its oral origins. The midrashim had a prehistory as actual sermons, and in their homey diction and their lively imagery they often strive toward a literary recreation of the living immediacy of the preacher addressing his congregation. Thus the rabbinic classics possess what could be called a vernacular-like character, for all their manifest status as literary texts. Mendele turned this vernacular-like character to artistic account in creating a credible theatrical voice for his itinerant bookseller-narrator who reports on life in the Pale. A generation later, Gnessin tapped the more subdued and reflective elements of speech in rabbinic Hebrew to evoke persuasively the rhythms of inner speech of characters who would actually have been thinking in Russian or Yiddish.

Conventional wisdom associates the rise of the novel elsewhere with a bold new embrace of the vernacular in narrative prose. It is a formula that in England has always worked well enough for Defoe and Richardson, but only marginally for Sterne and not at all for Fielding. Reading European and American novelistic prose in the light of the seemingly anomalous example of Hebrew, one notices more readily that the language of realism is only rarely a performance of the vernacular but is typically a complex system of *equivalences* for the vernacular that includes only local citation of and oblique allusion to actual spoken usage. Indeed, it is by no means a simple or natural operation to appropriate the vernacular for literary purposes, as the example of the nineteenth-century American novel before Mark Twain will suggest. The mediation of literary models to show how the vernacular can be used is usually indispensable.

In Hebrew, the first generation since ancient times of writers who were native speakers of the language became active in the 1940s (the so-called Palmach Generation). One might have thought that their prose would exhibit a new colloquial naturalness; but as the Israeli critic Gershon Shaked has persuasively demonstrated, Palmach Generation writing tends to be self-consciously "literary" in the pejorative sense, abounding in mannered locutions, rhetorical insistences, and replications of the clichés of European and American prose. It is only with more recent writers like Shabtai, Ben-Ner, Amalia Kahana-Carmon, the mature Amos Oz, and the later Yehoshua that Hebrew prose attains the subtlety and suppleness it reached by the early decades of this century among its best practitioners in European centers like Odessa, Vilna, Vienna, Berlin, and Paris. And most instructively, the prose of the finest contemporaries begins to sound more like that of the anti-*nusakh* current at the turn of the century than of their immediate predecessors in Israeli fiction.

This strange episode in literary history leads one to ponder the relation between language and national consciousness, on the one hand, and language and the representation of reality, on the other. By all rights, Hebrew on the threshold of the modern era should have been a dead language, or at any rate a purely academic or clerical one. The quixotic effort, improbably crowned with success, to create an "as-if" Hebrew world in fiction on European soil demonstrates that at least for this intellectual elite the Hebrew of the classical texts presented not a fossilized past but a crystallized living reality. The language potently persisted in their minds as the timeless, distinctive, and authoritative language of the Jewish people, and so it could become the solid basis of a new collective existence, of a cogent cultural nationalism, before Zionism was conceived.

The general principle of literary expression manifested in their enterprise is that literary realism is by no means dependent on a transcription of living speech but, on the contrary, always needs the stylistic norms and conventions of antecedent literature in order to achieve its compelling approximations of immediate experience. The success of the early modern Hebrew writers, working without a vernacular base, reveals something of how written language, in all its powerful internal cohesiveness as a formal system evolving through time and accumulating historical associations, may be deployed to evoke the feel and weight and complexity of the real world.

4/ FOGEL AND THE FORGING OF A HEBREW SELF

The fact that David Fogel has come to be seen, quite posthumously, as a pioneer of modernism in Hebrew poetry and, still more recently, as an innovative figure in early twentieth-century Hebrew fiction, should not deter us from the perception that his literary and linguistic enterprise was a most peculiar one. In part it was a peculiarity common to all Hebrew literature written in Europe, but Fogel pushed the paradox at the root of this whole cultural project to an ultimate extreme. No text he produced is more instructive in this regard than the diary he kept intermittently from September 1912, when he was twenty-one, until August 1922. There is no indication in the diary itself that he ever intended it for publication: it would only appear in print a quarter of a century after his murder by the Nazis in 1944, in a somewhat bowdlerized periodical version, and is now available in the more reliable edition of Mena-khem Perry (*Taḥanot Kavot*, Tel Aviv, 1990).

The linguistic oddness of Fogel's undertaking, as well as what I would regard as its linguistic achievement, is worth considering in detail. As a late adolescent, he had followed the path of many European-izing Jewish intellectuals of Orthodox upbringing: had left his native Russian *shtetl*, made his way to the big city (in this case, Vilna), abandoned religious observance, experienced an autodidact's introduction to European culture, and undergone his sexual initiation (for him, a rather complicated one, becoming the lover of an older woman who would soon seem repulsive to him in the midst of his persistent infatuation with her eleven-year-old daughter). This whole period of crucial transition was recorded by Fogel in a diary that he says, at the beginning of the text that has survived, was stolen from him. The diary that disappeared might have been written in either Hebrew or Yiddish, but Hebrew seems the more likely candidate because he mentions that he was making concerted efforts to perfect his Hebrew during his sojourn in Vilna. Now, in September 1912, he is back temporarily in his native Satanov, and thoroughly disgruntled to be there, weaving plans to move on to a truly "Western" city, Vienna (where he would arrive in mid-December), and in accordance beginning to teach himself German. A certain tension between his loyalty to Hebrew and the urgency of his mastering German is felt in several entries. He is afraid, he notes in the late fall of 1912, that his Hebrew may be slipping away from him, yet he has no choice but to concentrate on German. Within a few months he will be reading the leading European writers of the day—Ibsen, Hamsun, Maeterlinck—in German translation, but with some misgivings about his neglect of Hebrew. "I thirst—in the idiom of the *maskilim* of the well-known type—for knowledge, for light . . . the day is short and there is so much to do. I am now entering a world that is foreign to me, entering a foreign way of life and a foreign tongue—a period of transition. I regret my Hebrew language, having nothing with which to nourish it; I have no Hebrew books" (April 12, 1913). It is worth noting that Fogel, even at the tender age of twenty-two, interposes a certain ironic distance between himself and the prototypical *maskilim*, proponents of Hebrew Enlightenment, even as he seems to be following their program of supreme devotion to the ennobling force of European culture. His own project was really not Enlightenment in character, but for better (in terms of authenticity) and for worse (in terms of personal anguish) modernist, as I shall try to show.

Fogel's attachment to Hebrew was neither sentimental nor nationalist, and it is something of a puzzle why this profoundly isolated, neurasthenic, desperately unhappy young man trying to find a place for himself in Vienna should have chosen to record his most intimate thoughts in a language he had almost no occasion to speak, whose revival as a vernacular was being undertaken elsewhere. In Vienna, certainly in comparison with Vilna, there was hardly a Hebrew literary milieu he could have entered, nor would there be later in Paris where he took up residence in the mid-1920s, still pursuing his anomalous vocation as a Hebrew poet and writer of fiction. Fogel, moreover, unlike most of his fellow Hebraists in the early decades of the century, was not a committed Zionist, and indeed, every ideological movement repelled this fundamentally apolitical person: "I am especially disgusted and infuriated by the contact with those superior creatures who aspire to redeem the world. These people, who would set the world straight, how much unnaturalness and falseness they have in their make-up. They are antipathetic from head to toe" (August 13, 1918). When Fogel began the diary, he was not yet a poet, not even clearly aware that this was what he should or could become, though he does express vague literary ambitions, and by the end of the period covered in the diary he was producing important poems (a process unfortunately not dealt with in the text of the diary).

It may be best to begin an explanation of Fogel's embrace of Hebrew in negative terms. No European language — Russian, German, or, later, French — could have served as his medium of expression because he was not sufficiently at home in any of them. Yiddish, the one obviously viable alternative to Hebrew for the young Fogel, lacked the aura of literary prestige, especially for a writer with his aestheticizing bent, and was no doubt too much associated with the world of pious earlocks and dirty caftans and musty prayer rooms that he wanted to put behind him. There were, of course, talented young writers at precisely this moment who shared Fogel's European and modernist agenda and yet were not in the least troubled by such negative associations as they adopted Yiddish for their literary ambitions. Fogel himself, for reasons that are not entirely clear, switched to Yiddish around 1942 when he composed the fictionalized diary that was his last sustained text. But it is reasonable to infer that the young Fogel shared the pre-disposition of the Hebraists in the early modern era to see Hebrew as the one indigenous Jewish language that had an unambiguous claim to the status of high culture.

The Haskalah, for over a century before Fogel's birth, had dreamed of a secular Hebrew literature that would take its place among the culturally "advanced" literatures of Europe. In his strange way, Fogel carries forward this project, though with none of the naiveté or optimism of the Haskalah. Paradoxical though it may sound, he chooses Hebrew because it is the one avenue open to him for being European, for joining European high culture. Indeed, his incorrigible Europeanness is no less determinative of his identity than that of his exact Germanophone coeval, Walter Benjamin: both men in the end perished because they could not manage to extricate themselves, even as the clouds of destruction gathered, from the European setting they had made their only conceivable theater of operation.

I do not want to pretend that Fogel's diary is one of the great unknown documents of self-exploration of modern European literature. It is too raspingly complaining, too drearily repetitious for that, too clotted with scores upon scores of sentences that are mere variations of the following: "My condition is very bad; I sense that my powers are dwindling more and more from one day to the next, that I become weaker from one moment to the next — and there is no way out" (February 8, 1913). There are, one must grant, passages in which the diarist comes to startling insights into himself and his relations with others, but what I think is truly compelling about Fogel's diary is the palpable feeling it conveys of fashioning a living language, a language that, though not the writer's actual vernacular, is able to trace the twisting contours of his inner life, body forth a thoroughly modern and European sense of self and other, motive and identity.

For a Hebrew reader at the end of the twentieth century, Fogel's language in most respects sounds remarkably contemporary. There are, of course, peculiar little archaisms as well as occasional lexical or idiomatic innovations of Fogel's that never caught on and that hence merely seem odd now. But the basic patterns of syntax, the terms used for self-analysis and moral experience, what I would call the rhythms of conceptualization of this prose, still have considerable immediacy, and by no means sound quaint. It is worth trying to understand how this could be.

The sharp introspection that is the very purpose of this text repeatedly leads the writer to attend minutely to the fluctuations of his own physical and spiritual condition and to select with precision from the available Hebrew lexicon — rich enough, even then, in regard to representing inner states and symptomology — for rendering that condition: "Illnesses, too, have swooped down on me. One illness includes them all. That weakness in the limbs and slackness of the mind. Incessant headache. And the desire for life I had within me, despite all those contortions and grimaces, is draining away. Apathy to everything" (February 23, 1918). Although general Hebrew usage in the three-quarters of a century since these lines were written has traversed the distance, say, from Defoe's English to ours, the language here sounds strikingly natural, virtually contemporary. The vocabulary, moreover, is all indigenously Hebrew, the sole loanword, "apathy" (apatia), a borrowing that still has currency today.

As a writer of prose fiction, Fogel would attain complexly orchestrated effects of considerable subtlety — adumbrated in the diary in a couple of descriptive passages — but what is arresting about his language of introspection is its simplicity and directness. When he needs to conceptualize inner life, he makes the most ordinary Hebrew terms serve admirably, and his notation of inner tensions has the transparency of the notation of pieces moved on a checkerboard. Thus, he contrasts his sense of himself when he was in Vilna and now in Satanov: "My soul [then] was not flawed, and it left its imprint in all my behavior; I always knew myself, this self of mine [ha'ani sheli], and ever since I left there, I haven't known myself; I am not I" (13 Tishrei 5673 [September 1912]). I don't know who was the first to use the first-person singular pronoun 'ani with the definite article in front of it as a noun meaning "the self," but it could not have been very common in the Hebrew of 1912. Although it is philosophically suspect to call any linguistic practice "natural," Fogel's promotion of "I" to "self" has an *air* of naturalness: he requires a term to designate "self" in distinction to soul, consciousness, mind, and without the slightest neologizing strain, almost as though the term with that acceptation were already fully established in the language, he adopts the ordinary *'ani* for his purpose.

Linguistic usage follows the lead of introspective perception. What makes Fogel a modernist even before he has imbibed the new works of European modernist literature is his sense that the self is not whole, or one, or reliably continuous. (There are manifold expressions of just this sense in European literature on the verge of World War I: its most subtle and densely complex articulation was achieved by Proust in precisely the time span that Fogel was writing his diary.) The language of estrangement from self, of inner division, crops up again and again in the diary. "I am not I," he says here boldly but strikingly, and elsewhere (in a prison camp for alien subjects during the war), "I don't know myself. Fogel has lost Fogel" (June 1, 1915). When he has not lost himself, he perceives a violent succession of selves destroying each other in turn: "This David tramples on the grave of the previous David. There are no remnants from yesterday. . . . I am walking into an abyss of darkness and chaos, constantly walking onward. And alone, alone" (July 22, 1914). Again and again, he exhibits an ability to make the simplest Hebrew words serve to represent a process of self-alienation in virtually spatial terms: "I have gone out of myself. By entering into another. I have become outside [*na'aseiti huts*]. And there is no inside" (May 25, 1919).

Fogel's relentless self-observation leads him to a language that persuasively encompasses psychological patterns or, if you will, psychodynamics, without recourse to any technical terminology. Thus, in a long reflection on his affair with the older woman he designates as Ts., he notes the following about his own motives and feelings: "at a time when life in Vilna had already made me a despairing pessimist . . . I needed to become intoxicated on the one hand, in order to forget reality, and on the other hand—I needed the soft and warm caress of a mother, a sheltering wing. I was alone and abandoned and suffering—and I thought to find a good mother in Ts., an instrument of intoxication, oblivion, healing–in her warm body" (9 Heshvan 5673 [November 1912]). I suspect that behind Fogel's formulation here, whether consciously or not, is Bialik's perennially popular poem, *Hakhnisini taḥat kenafeikh* ("Take me under your wing / And be for me mother and sister"), though it does not really operate as a literary allusion, for Fogel has taken apart the elements of the sheltering mother imagery and reassembled them as a literal representation of his sexual involvement with Ts.

A little later in the same entry, as Fogel reflects on the rapid and extreme devolution of his relationship with his first mistress, one palpably senses his careful selection of terms to define the refractory nature of the moral and psychological phenomenon he is reporting:

> She was no longer the beloved Ts., for whom you tremble with love, or more precisely, with lust, when you recall her, but the hated, despised Ts., whose recollection causes anguish, and the necessity of hatred causes anguish. Yes, last year at this time I was filled with regret and suffered terribly for hating her, for not being able to dismiss her and consider her dead. Half a year I lived with her; I quarreled and was reconciled with her and again we lived together. We spent the entire winter in quarrels and reconciliations and the intoxication of sexual lust.

All this is reported with a lexical precision to which my translation barely does justice. The "quarrels" (or perhaps better, "squabbles") is not the weightier *riv* or *merivah* but *qetatah*, with its connotation of pettiness, just the right term for a fatiguing, spiteful, frictional falling out of once passionate lovers. A long time ago in Hebrew, there had not been a sharp demarcation between love, *'ahavah* and lust, *ta'avah*. In the story of Amnon and Tamar (2 Samuel 13), the verb *'ahav*, which elsewhere in the Bible means love, clearly refers to a condition of lust. By the early twentieth century, love and lust in Hebrew had definitely become distinct terms–perhaps under the influence of the moral semantics of European languages, though that is a conjecture that could be confirmed only through documented philological investigation. (The verb that is cognate with *ta'avah, hit'avah*, remains morally neutral, simply meaning "to want.") In any case, it is patent that the distinction between love and lust is essential for Fogel, who does not want any blurry idealizing vocabulary to misrepresent the actual nature of what he has experienced. To reinforce this distinction, in the last two words of the passage quoted Fogel couples *ta'avah* with *min*, "sex," again a relatively precocious usage of a Hebrew term that previously meant "kind" or "gender," in precisely the sense of libidinal relation that the equivalent abstraction has in the various European languages.

His account reads so smoothly and aptly that in a way it seems quite unexceptional, but I think we need to remind ourselves how exceptional this in fact must have been in Hebrew eighty years ago. A twenty-one-year-old refugee from the world of Orthodoxy, not entirely confident that his recent efforts to consolidate his literary Hebrew have given him a real mastery of the language, is able to record what he has undergone morally and psychologically in prose that is nicely discriminating, unstrained, and quite free of the fustian and the ostentatiously allusive rhetoric so common in the Hebrew of the period. (This last feature must owe a good deal to the young Fogel's reading of anti-*nusakh* writers — especially Gnessin, I would guess — but his own linguistic intuition is nevertheless remarkable.) What this means is that Fogel at twenty-one had already found a way of thinking about himself as a European person — not filtering his experience through Bible and Talmud and Hasidic homily but observing, with the appropriate lexical terms, how his first sexual partner offered him an ambiguous mixture of physical rapture and maternal warmth, how lust became hatred, how the hatred itself proved to be not a simple emotion as it roused in him resentment over his incapacity to feel detachment from her. Fogel at this early moment does not yet imagine becoming a writer of fiction, but one can already glimpse here the future author of the fine novella on the depredations of erotic life, *Facing the Sea*, as well as of the somewhat less focused novella, *In the Sanitarium*, and the intriguing if psychologically overwrought novel, *Married Life*.

The Hebrew literary tradition, in some ways from the Bible onward and certainly from the rabbinic period onward through its multiple historical offshoots, is by and large strongly tilted toward collective experience, often inclined to see the individual as a prototype or spokesman for the collective. It is hardly an accident that the first truly artful fiction in modern Hebrew, the stories and novels of S. Y. Abramowitz (the latter of course reworked from the Yiddish) use a prototypical narrating persona, Mendele the Bookseller, and take as their subject *kelal Yisrael*, collective Jewish existence in the Pale of Settlement. Against this whole tradition, the young Fogel counterposes a stubborn perception that no individual's experience is reducible to common denominators and collective terms: Walter Benjamin said of the novel that it deals with the "incommensurability" of individual existence, and that is quite how Fogel sees it. In a 1913 entry, after having received a letter from Ts.'s daughter, now in America, exhorting him not to think of death—he had at least toyed with the idea of suicide—because he had not yet drunk from the cup of life, he reflects as follows: " 'the cup of life'—a worn-out phrase! Why haven't I drunk from the cup of life?! I am now twenty-two, and in these few years I have lived more than other people do in their whole lives. I have drunk from the cup of life: I have suffered. There is no cup of life but rather cups of life, for every individual—a special one different from the next. I have drunk a large, full cup" (February 8, 1913).

Examining the bitter but interesting contents of that cup is not only the underlying motive for writing the diary but also the exacting activity that determines the innovative shape of its prose. I would like to quote one somewhat longer passage in order to illustrate how this process works, how Fogel's Hebrew develops what I called earlier a distinctive "rhythm of conceptualization." I have preserved his somewhat eccentric sentence divisions and concomitant punctuation because they are essential manifestations of that rhythm. The entry was made about a month after his release from detention camp in the summer of 1916, and turns on his initial involvement with the woman who was to become his first wife.

> Now a strange young woman has attached herself to me. Ilka. Consumptive and sickly. And I find that I like her. And I'm very sorry for her. Because who am I?! Shattered. A lad whose juices have dried up. And I'm not capable of loving at all. And her in particular. And I go walking with

her long and short and feel an inner closeness to her and enjoy her childish way of talking. Yet when she's not with me, I feel a secret fear of her.
A fear that is unclear to me. Perhaps her consumption causes it. I feel
death in her. And out of compassion I draw close to her and also show her
signs of affection. – Is that all? Life is inscrutable to me. I stand before it
wondering and uncomprehending. As though I had just descended from
some other planet. I understand nothing. You walk around . . . stand still
. . . run. Conversation with people etc. – I understand nothing. Like an
infant. Why and for what??? And even terror does not grip me. And a consumptive young woman loves me. Swarthy. Not pretty. Not ugly. Loves
and suffers and suffers. And I don't love and suffer and suffer. And I understand nothing. (August 11, 1916)

What is most remarkable about this passage – and there are a good
many others like it in the diary – is that Fogel, evidently writing only
for himself, in an effort to make some sense of his own experience,
flatly ignores the decorum of literary Hebrew in order to make the language fit the disjunctive nature of his thought and feeling. The most
salient expression of this swerve from precedent is the use of a staccato series of fragmentary phrases. The prose is neither paratactic nor
hypotactic but atomistic, articulated as a chain of brief non-sentences
and sentences, many of them only one or two or three words long, separated from each other by the full stop of periods or sometimes question marks. What leads Fogel to do this? As he watches himself, scru-
tinizes his fears and desires, nothing has necessary connection,
nothing has dependable coherence, contradictions abound, and the assurance of connexity implicit in conventional syntax must be abandoned. Ilka as he tries to encompass her in his imagination is not an
intelligible whole, not Ilka, who is such and such, in the tidy subordination of a dependent clause. Instead, in stroboscopic discontinuity,
she is: Ilka. Consumptive. Swarthy. Not pretty. Not ugly. Loves and
suffers. The same discontinuity and impenetrability are manifested in
Fogel's perception of his own feelings: he wonders, for example,
whether he is drawn to Ilka out of the fear, and attraction, of death she
rouses in him, and moments later in the concatenation of fragmentary
utterances he announces that he feels no fear. If elsewhere he empha-
sizes the incommensurability of his life-experience with anyone

else's, here he goes still further and asserts that this incommensurable stuff is also unintelligible to himself (another notion Walter Benjamin attaches to the novelistic sense of life, *perplexity*, is apposite here). Thus life itself seems to him inscrutable or impenetrable (*setumim*), and he imagines himself as an alien not in the national but in the science fiction sense, dropped from another planet and baffled by the workings of the one on which he finds himself.

In terms of literary form, this staccato prose – fashioned, by a gracious coincidence of the zeitgeist, at the very moment Joyce was laboring on *Ulysses* – represents an incipient stream of consciousness. I don't think Fogel actually had any literary models for it. The one deployment of a form of interior monologue that he was most likely to have encountered, in the Hebrew novellas of U. N. Gnessin, works with long paratactic sentences that produce an opposite effect. His approximation, however, of stream of consciousness is dictated by a motive at least in part akin to Joyce's: a desire to make language intimate the immediacy and disjunctiveness of mental process, make it convey the way that experience bombards consciousness with so many pellets of discrete data that it may threaten to become unmanageable.

When Fogel began to experiment with prose fiction, only three years after the last entry in the diary, he did not adopt any technique of stream of consciousness. In the handful of fictional texts he actually produced, the interiority of the protagonists is definitely the focus of representation, but his aspiration to turn out finely wrought aesthetic wholes led him away from fragmentation and toward a version of *style indirect libre* in which he could achieve a supple interweave of outer and inner, scene and subjectivity, narratorial authority and the emotional fluctuations of the fictional personages. In regard to these narrative procedures, too, the early diary proves retrospectively to be not only a laboratory for self-exploration but a technical testing-ground for the future writer of fiction. Indeed, for someone with literary ambitions, the two impulses are hard to separate: fictional invention itself is another vehicle of self-knowledge, a way of recasting one's experience under the camouflage of fabulation; and, correspondingly, even so scrupulous an effort to observe what one had undergone as we find in Fogel's diary is also on some level a playing with the possibility of turning it into literature.

One very early entry, from the fall of 1912, vividly illustrates this delicate interplay between the aim of self-articulation and the aim of literary representation. The young Fogel, just back from his year in Vilna, is much preoccupied with the erotically charged, now forever frustrated relationship he had there with the pubescent Haniah. Now he tries to capture one resonant and representative moment in that relationship, prefacing the entry with the notation, "something from my past." The realization of scene, the minute and subtle attention to physical details, are qualities relatively rare in the published Hebrew fiction available in 1912; and the atmospheric treatment of the scene, the way it is made to appear suffused with feeling, intricately mirroring the emotions of the principal actor and his fraught relationship with the young girl, is a remarkable anticipation of the accomplished narrative art, twenty years later, of *Facing the Sea*. There are, to be sure, a few clumsy elements of repetition in the choice of language, and perhaps the lexicon of the emotions is somewhat wanting at a couple of points, but the evocativeness of the writing already looks forward to the Fogel who would be the last European master of Hebrew prose. His conscious intention in this passage is of course to "recapture" an experience that has moved him, but he imagines it novelistically, conceives all its defining features in the narratological and stylistic terms of the fiction he has been reading. Here, without further comment, are the last three quarters of the entry dated 20 Heshvan 5673:

> Within the room the clock ticks distinctly, outside drops run off from the roof at brief intervals and fall into the puddles making bubbles. – I sit at the table studying a book. The table is covered with a soiled tablecloth – the right corner serves me as a bookshelf, several books stacked one on top of another upon it – the middle part is my desk, and at the left corner an old newspaper is spread out over the tablecloth, and on it is set a glass in a saucer, at the bottom of which are the lees of tea. The clock ticks and

the drops fall, and in the room a mute, gentle, pleasant sadness hovers. In the courtyard slow steps sound; I recognize them. The door opens slowly and deliberately; the girl enters. I do not hasten to turn my head toward her because I know it is she and no one else who has come in. The girl says good evening to my landlady, approaches me slowly, emits a slightly choked hello as she thrusts her cool hand into mind. I indicate to her a place to sit on the bench that stands between the wall separating the kitchen from the second room and the stove – lengthwise – and between my table, to the right of it, and the wall – breadthwise; the bench is where I sleep. The girl sits down unobtrusively – and is silent. I continue to study the book; I have to finish the passage, and she sits to my right, musing about something or other, giving off a scent of outdoors, wet and rain-soaked. I finish the passage, turn to the girl and begin to speak with her confidentially. I look at her dreamy eyes, her dark-blue hat, the collar of her red sweater and her short gymnasium-student's skirt. We whisper and whisper. There is a dim light in the room and on the wall to my right the shadow of my long-haired head and the girl's shadow sway together. And the girl tells me in a quiet nervous voice how her ill-spirited jealous mother torments her for coming to see me, how she humiliates and insults her, – and the girl quietly bemoans her situation, and her shadow slowly sways on the wall – and I listen and feel an inward pressure of sorrow, tenderness, melting compassion. I comfort her, console her, tell her reassuring things. The girl is a bit encouraged and smiles a little, like the smile of a sunset on a winter day, over snow. And everything in the room expresses mute and pleasant melancholy, – everything: the dim light and the smoky glass, the dusty mirror by the books – and the books, the bench and the folded bedding at its head, the silent souls and their shadows, the single window covered with a curtain halfway up, and in its upper half the black night peers in and the window of the house opposite and the pail of water by the window. The girl remains silent, looking at me devotedly and hopefully, and I look at her with paternal love. Thus we go on sitting. . . .

5

THE INNER
IMMIGRATION OF
HEBREW PROSE

The great wave of emigration from Eastern Europe that began after 1881 was, of course, overwhelmingly a movement to the West and particularly to America. Individual Hebrew writers were swept along in this broad movement but almost always against the promptings of their interior compass as writers. Ideology, sociology, and literary history conspired to make the New World an uncongenial landscape for Hebrew novelists and poets; and with very rare exceptions, their efforts to acclimate Hebrew literature to the American scene were strained, self-conscious, and artistically unconvincing. Hebrew literature, to be sure, has often proved to be an extraordinarily supple instrument of assimilation, making it possible for Jews to absorb and affirm as Jews highly divergent and often seemingly alien cultural values from their various host nations — in medieval Spain, in Renaissance Italy, in Enlightenment Germany, in prerevolutionary Russia, and elsewhere, earlier and farther afield.

The obvious historical reason why this process never took place with any notable success in America is that by the time the Jewish immigration to America was fully under way, the nucleus of an autonomous Hebrew community in Palestine had been created which made the American route seem from the Hebraist point of view like a great detour destined never to return to the main road. At the beginning of the 1920s, after the Russian Revolution had essentially cut off Hebrew literature in Eastern Europe, the Hebrew literary center shifted decisively to Palestine; by the end of that decade, the altogether improbable enterprise of reviving Hebrew as a spoken language was also firmly established; and by virtue of this whole portentous historical transition, Hebrew literature in America was condemned to peripherality as the anomalous vestige of a European cultural and linguistic pluralism that had no real counterpart in the New World. And yet, Hebrew writing in America does offer occasional tantalizing glimpses of that classical dynamism of assimilatory power operating even in this country, against the logic of historical circumstances, and I shall presently turn to one important text which is exemplary in precisely this regard.

In order to understand the problematic nature of the Hebrew writer's imaginative relation to America, we should keep in mind certain essential features of the social context of Hebrew literature in Europe and its linguistic peculiarity, especially in contradistinction to Yiddish literature. Hebrew literature, from Mendelssohn's Berlin to the Odessa of Ahad Ha'am, was an elite movement, its constituency in Eastern Europe composed typically of refugees from the intelligentsia of Orthodox Jewry – half-secularized ex-yeshiva students, their bellies full of the Talmud and its commentaries, their heads humming with biblical verses, who sought to be at once enlightened moderns and aristocratically proud Jews by nurturing a literature written in a language neither they nor anyone else actually spoke. This literature lived through tiny, intense coteries in centers like Vilna, Warsaw, Lemberg, Odessa (and, after the Revolution, briefly and fitfully, Berlin and Paris). The literary miscellanies through which it characteristically propagated itself had subscribers that in any given instance numbered no more than a thousand or so, often only a few hundred.

Now, the stereotypical notion that all East European Jews three or four generations ago lived in *shtetlakh* is of course misconceived because there was in fact a large Jewish urban population (without prior urban experience, the character of New York's immigrant Jewish community, for example, would have been quite different from what it was). But, peculiarly, for the creators of modern Hebrew literature in Russia, Poland, and Galicia, that stereotype generally holds; the vast majority of the Hebrew writers came from the Jewish townlets. The biography of the great poet, Haim Nahman Bialik, is paradigmatic: he grew up in a little village in the Russian province of Vohlin in the 1870s; as an adolescent of extraordinary intellectual gifts, was sent to the famous yeshiva at Volozhin; was infected by the new spirit of Enlightenment, abandoned the yeshiva, and naturally gravitated to the Hebrew center of Odessa. Why the Hebrew movement should have chiefly attracted young men from *shtetl* backgrounds is not entirely clear, though one basic fact of literary sociology may offer a partial explanation: would-be writers with personal roots in the Jewish urban proletariat were far more likely to choose Yiddish as their medium, for by writing in Hebrew, they would have cut themselves off from their own social origins as well as from their most natural audience. The Hebrew Enlightenment, by contrast, was at least to some degree a clandestine movement out in the provinces, the handful of *maskilim* in any small town sharing the pages of those forbidden Hebrew periodicals and imagining for themselves a literary audience of like-minded daring souls elsewhere in the Hebrew "underground," in a way writing consciously more for *netzah yisrael*, Eternal Israel, than for the masses of contemporary Jewry.

This problematic obliquity of relation to modern reality was especially poignant for Hebrew writers of prose fiction. From the beginnings of modern Hebrew fiction in the early nineteenth century, writers were compelled to create what Dov Sadan has called an "as-if" world, rendering – in both narration and dialogue – the lives of characters who actually would have been speaking Yiddish, German, Russian, or Polish in a purely literary language intricately patched together out of the beautiful scraps of sacred texts. The first phase of this literature typically used biblical vocabulary, grammar, and syntax; when Hebrew prose came of age with Mendele's shift from Yiddish to Hebrew in the 1880s, it turned to the more supple syntax and the much vaster lexicon of rabbinic Hebrew. What I should like to stress is that both these major historical phases of Hebrew were the products of an agrarian society. The relatively distanced, lofty, poetic language of the Bible frequently led writers to the cultivation of pastoral themes, not only in the 'lyric poetry but also in some of the prose. (The first Hebrew novel, we might recall, Mapu's *The Love of Zion*, published in 1853, is a romantic pastoral set in the time of Isaiah.) The more particularizing language of the Mishnah and the Midrash, on the other hand, was surprisingly well suited, as the genius of Mendele brilliantly demonstrated, for a realistic representation of life in the small towns of the Pale of Settlement. This Hebrew shaped in Palestine under the Greeks and the Romans was discovered to possess rich resources for rendering a smithy hammering at his anvil, a housewife stirring her fire-blackened pots, a conclave of study-house loafers analyzing the wealth of the Rothschilds in the manner of Rashi on the Pentateuch. It was quite another matter, however, to fashion an adequate literary expression for the nervous rhythm of café life in the big cities, the massive clamor of industrial machinery and what it did to the people who operated it, the sense of enormous size and teeming variety of the modern metropolis.

Dov Sadan has proposed that the whole practice of writing into existence an "as-if" Hebrew reality led writers by imperceptible stages to Zionism, to the dream of creating a living community where linguistic "as if" would be turned into cultural "is." I would like to suggest further that the *representational bias* of the Hebrew medium also tilted writers toward a historical reality in Palestine which was for the most part still agrarian (and certainly agrarian in ideological principle), and where even what passed for a city, Jerusalem, could be written about, as Y. H. Brenner showed in *Breakdown and Bereavement* (1918), as a kind of extension of the *shtetl*. It would of course be crassly reductive to say that Hebrew writers turned to the Zionist ideal out of purely literary considerations; but writers in general are impelled, together with whatever other motives they may have, by an instinct to go where their language can most readily take hold. And for Hebrew novelists and short-story writers, that was in Jaffa and Jerusalem and the Valley of Jezreel, not in the streets of Manhattan.

For the setting of Jewish immigrant life in America offered above all a densely concentrated, fiercely intense urban experience which was largely outside the imaginative ken and at first beyond the linguistic reach of Hebrew literature. Repeated efforts were made to recreate in New York, and even in Boston and Chicago, the sort of Hebrew literary life that writers had known in Odessa and Vilna; short-lived periodicals were established as early as the 1880s; little publishing houses were founded. Hebrew publishing and periodicals persist in this country on a very small scale to the present, but it is fair enough to say that no American Hebrew press has had a fraction of the impact of Stiebel in Berlin or of the Brothers and Widow Ramm in Vilna, and no American Hebrew journal a fraction of the importance of the Odessa *Ha-Shiloah* or the Viennese *Bikkurei ha-'Ittim*. The fervent devotion of Hebraists in America to the cause of Hebrew culture is an impressive human phenomenon, but the prevailing sense among writers has been that their cause was embattled, perhaps altogether desperate. Yitzhak Rabinowitz (1846–1900), a minor poet who arrived in New York in the early 1890s, in the first surge of immigration from Russia, is a touching case in point.

Writing in Hebrew in the spring of 1893 to a friend in Russia, he observes, with a sardonic play on a phrase from Deuteronomy used to express the accessibility of the Torah, "Our Hebrew language – it is not on the other side of the sea. Here no one recognizes it. . . . Our brethren here do not read Hebrew at all. Here the jargon maidservant [Yiddish, of course] has taken over the place of the mistress, Hebrew." And, with an edge of elitist disdain characteristic of the early modern Hebraists, Rabinowitz goes on to express his disgust with the flourishing world of Yiddish journalism that had taken root in New York: "Here, whoever wants to assume the title of a jargon editor is free to do so. . . . No breadth of understanding or insight is required. A bit of stupidity, frivolity, levity, mockery, a few trumped-up lies, and you have sufficient bricks and mortar for the building of a jargon publication." In this particular letter, Rabinowitz stresses the fact that in the New World there was no social milieu to sustain Hebrew. Addressing the same friend four years later (July 9, 1897), he also intimates that the very urban setting was inimical to the Hebrew muse. "It is five years since my hard fate cast me to the other side of the sea. I have not dipped quill in ink to write anything or roused my lyre for any of the periodicals or annuals published in Europe. . . . I have grown old and gray [he had just passed his fiftieth year], and as I dwell in this desert of nations here in New York, the metropolis of arrogant gentiles, a place where sacred stones are spilled out at every street corner, my inspiration has vanished." (The Rabinowitz letters are quoted in Y. Kabokov, *Halutzei hasifrut ha'ivrit be'Amerika*, Tel Aviv, 1966, pp. 306 and 215.)

Where the very pavement of the city streets seemed to resist the outpourings of lyric pathos and rhapsody that were characteristic of early modern Hebrew literature, it is not surprising that some of the immigrant Hebrew poets should have tried to discover on these shores a new kind of pastoral landscape, producing quasi-epic or balladic lucubrations on Indian and Negro life. Such dalliance with American exotica was of course a self-conscious act of willed acculturation, a symptom of the problem rather than a solution to it. Throughout the period of the great immigration, prose fiction, the medium best suited to a mimetic engagement of the urban reality that the immigrant Jews actually lived in, was limited to characteristically schematic and tendentious short stories, often with the burden of complaining about the hostility of the New World environment to authentic Jewish values. It is instructive that the first Hebrew novel written in America and about life in America, Simon Halkin's *Yehiel ha-Hagri* (roughly, Yehiel Immigrantov), did not appear until 1929. Halkin's career is a fascinating intersection of different cultural forces, and it is worth considering in some detail.

Halkin arrived in New York in 1914 at the age of sixteen, accompanied by his parents and his younger brother Abraham, who was to become a prominent Jewish historian. From the family background in White Russia, he brought with him an acute sense of the spiritual power of Hasidism; from his father, a strong attachment to Hebrew and to the various branches of traditional Jewish learning. He was young enough to complete a university education in this country (at

New York University); to achieve an idiomatic mastery of English and with that, a deep responsiveness to English Romantic poetry, to Whitman (whom he would later translate into Hebrew), Emerson, Joyce, D. H. Lawrence, and Thomas Wolfe. Halkin's choice of Hebrew rather than English as his medium of literary expression is associated, understandably, with an increasingly emphatic commitment to Zionism (in 1932 he emigrated to Palestine; he was caught in America at the outbreak of the war in 1939 and ended up staying another ten years, until he was invited to occupy the chair of modern Hebrew literature at the Hebrew University in Jerusalem). What is interesting, however, about Halkin's literary activity in this country is that he never viewed America merely as an indifferent way station to Zion, whatever his belief that the new Hebrew center in Israel by an inexorable historical logic would be the only enduring center of Jewish existence.

Both Halkin's poetry and his fiction incorporate a complex sense of the American social scene, of this country's urban and rural landscapes, and of American literary culture. Although Halkin continued his activity as a poet, essayist, and translator after his move to Israel in 1949, his career as a novelist ended shortly before his emigration, with the publication in 1945 of *Toward Crisis ('Ad Mashber)*, his ambitious second novel set in New York at the end of the twenties. The earlier and slighter *Yehiel ha-Hagri* was a highly subjective, lyrical novel (directly influenced, I would assume, by *A Portrait of the Artist as a Young Man*) that brooded over the spiritual oscillations of a sensitive young man caught between the New World promise of stirring freedom of expression and the insistent mystical doctrine of his Hasidic antecedents. *Toward Crisis,* by contrast, is a more panoramic book that embraces an intricate network of social, moral, ideological, and theological problems faced by a variegated set of Jewish characters — radicals, bohemians, crass careerists, even an intellectual rabbi — deployed at various points in the physical and social geography of New York.

How did Halkin go about fashioning a Hebrew literary instrument adequate to this large task? In regard to narrative technique, he probably made some use of the model offered by the Russian-Hebrew novelist, Uri Nisan Gnessin, who was active in the first decade of this century; who in contrast to most of his Hebrew contemporaries, dealt with intellectual Jews in urban settings; and who developed a form of narrated monologue (that is, *style indirect libre*) which reproduced the slowly shifting rhythms and repetitions of mental life. The example of Gnessin's narrated monologue was in all likelihood reinforced and complicated by Halkin's acquaintance with the lyric novels of Thomas Wolfe. Stylistically, Halkin's long, sinuous sentences recall the shape of Gnessin's sentences and of Wolfe's, but the texture of his language derives from the Hebrew tradition of Mendele and the so-called *nusakh* writers who (unlike Gnessin) used a richly allusive language, which constantly and inventively exploited the idiom of classical Hebrew texts, often to ironic purpose.

I would like to draw particular attention to one arresting section of *Toward Crisis*, a twenty-five-page apostrophe to the city called "In Thy Midst, O New York"—a title which of course alludes to the Psalmist's phrase, "In thy midst, O Jerusalem." (Because it is an apostrophe, this section does not use the technique of narrated monologue prevalent elsewhere in the novel.) This rhapsodic-historical-analytical-satirical set piece, which strikes me as a remarkable document of American literature and not just of Hebrew literature in America, is perhaps the single moment when Hebrew prose succeeded in fully assimilating the new American world, just when the tide of history was carrying its practitioners to a very different horizon. As in earlier periods of Hebrew literature, back to the Renaissance and the Middle Ages, the "assimilation" of a particular world involves not merely a responsiveness to its look and feel but also the assimilation of its exemplary representations in the native literature. If Halkin's strategy for the narrative rendering of experience can be traced back to Gnessin and his highly wrought allusive prose to the school of Mendele, the celebratory mode of his great prose poem on New York, probably even something of its governing rhythms, would not have been possible without the example of Whitman.

"In Thy Midst, O New York" moves inward in concentric circles from a grand survey of the great cities of Western history to an evocation of the uniqueness among them of New York. Then, after several pages in which the strident, teeming, tempting, pulsating life of the city is conjured up, the speaker passes on to the Jews of New York and their extravagant love for the metropolis that has accorded them so unprecedented a welcome in their historical wanderings. The chapter concludes with a vignette of a Jewish student and his date, enraptured after a concert, cradling cheap coffee mugs in their hands as they sit in the bright light of an automat fervently discussing the advent of the classless society they will help bring about. Halkin's rhapsody ends, then, on a note of delicately poised irony. If I read him right, he sees the radicalism of these children of the immigrant generation as something quixotic, self-deluded, pregnant with painful consequences which they in their innocence do not yet guess; but it is also an expression of the enormous energy of idealism released by the manifold excitements and the new freedom of the great city.

What makes Halkin's Hebrew celebration of New York remarkable is the special resonances he produces by evoking the city's imposing presence through constant echoes of Hebrew tradition, the voices of the Psalmist and of Rabbi Akiva joining in chorus with that of Walt Whitman. To the literate Hebrew reader, there is a palpable element of sheer playfulness in this phrase-by-phrase recall of traditional texts, but for the most part, the echoes work to sustain and enlarge the idea of New York, not to undercut it ironically. Thus, the narrator affirms, "One must conclude [the talmudic *heveh 'omer*], every other great city in the world — the love for it is dependent on some concrete benefit: its beauty, its strength, its wisdom. But the love for you, New York, is altogether a love not dependent on concrete benefit." The pointed allusion here is to the rabbinic contrast between love for another person that is dependent on concrete gratification, *'ahavah hateluyah bedavar* (Amnon's lust for Tamar), and that which is disinterested (the love of David and Jonathan). In translation, I'm afraid, the distinctive blend of poignancy and affectionate humor of Halkin's allusive prose would require elaborate line-by-line annotation. I will try nevertheless to suggest something of the movement of his writing by offering in English a brief portion of one of his long, surging, Whit-

manesque lyric inventories. I have tried to indicate some of the specifically biblical resonances through the admittedly awkward device
of introducing anachronisms into the translation, more or less in
keeping with the King James Version. One may assume approximately
that what doesn't sound vaguely biblical is probably emphatically rabbinic in the original:

> By means of perception, New York, beyond the grasp of the physical
> senses, do your sons perceive your nature, and the stranger understan-
> deth not. When a foreigner enters your gates in a great ship creeping
> through your harbor like a giant brooding goose, he fixes external signs of
> recognition, as he is enjoined by the picture postcards – those frightful
> silhouettes piled up on the horizons of your skies – they are your tremen-
> dous buildings, the famous skyscrapers: those mighty violins playing
> him the melody of the New World as it is written in Baedeker – the bro-
> cade of your bridges, at once menaced and ethereal, and in like manner,
> other logical signs and wonders, offspring alien to your true nature, to
> your essential reality, as it were. Coming into your midst, he finds him-
> self dismayed and overwhelmed and he learns to walk, like a toddler,
> through the crowds of your central streets – and he begins to fix more dis-
> tinctive, more personal signs of you, through sight and smell and hear-
> ing: here are your hotels filled with glittering windows, each one of
> which is worth as much in windows as a whole city in the foreigner's
> homeland: and here are your theaters proudly builded and the shields of
> the mighty men do hang over their entrances, they are the many-colored
> garbs for the inclinations of man and the deeds of humankind both good
> and evil; these are your factories for furs and clothing, for men's apparel
> and women's garments, upper and under and in-between, and these are
> your warehouses for cloaks and robes, for shoes and sandals, for sox and
> stockings, for hats and caps and headgear, for pyjamas and bathing suits,
> cunning work in blue and crimson and scarlet thread, in the silk of Japan
> and the patterned linen of China; these are your restaurants, that make
> the longing eye ache with their show-windows, those storehouses con-
> taining every manner of bounty, and all the desires of the wastrel on-
> looker cannot match them, and these are your department stores, that by
> turns make the hand dance and paralyze it in the empty pocket with
> their mountains upon mountains of necessities for body and soul and
> luxuries for body and soul, that soar majestically in their dozens upon
> dozens of stories, and the stranger who draweth near to them with a still

empty pocket is forbidden to make use of them but may only behold. (P. 92)

And, pirouetting coyly on this last phrase, which in the Talmud refers to lighted Hanukah candles, the speaker goes on in pursuit of still other aspects of the inner radiance of the city which the mere stranger understandeth not.

The fictional time of the novel, let us remember, is the end of the 1920s, that transient moment bright with possibilities when the first American-born generation of Jews after the great immigration was just coming into its own and the shadow of the Depression had not yet descended. The time of writing is the mid-forties, when the whole world of European origins had just been irrevocably destroyed and Israel was desperately struggling to be born. Some of New York's Jews, like Halkin himself, would soon be joining the new Zionist state. For a good many others, the magnetism of the great metropolis would soon yield to the allure of more comfortable living in the suburbs, or in the Sun Belt to the west and the south. It was perhaps the last likely moment for a writer to express the passionate romance of the East European Jewish immigrants with New York. It is a peculiar irony of cultural history that this romance should have been given such plangent expression in of all languages Hebrew – a bold though solitary testimony to the dynamic interplay of cultures that took place so often elsewhere but in America was a consummation devoutly wished by the few and never fully achieved.

6

THE ISRAELI NOVEL AND POST–WORLD WAR II FICTION

L iterary history is an activity of definition and classification that almost always involves egregious imprecisions. It is also a necessary activity for the understanding of the relation between literature and culture, literature and the historical moment, for without its generalizations literary expression dissolves under inspection into a welter of unconnected individual texts, each a law unto itself. A hardheaded nominalist would say, with some justification, that there is no such thing as the Israeli novel and that a label like "post–World War II fiction," which must stretch over so many disparate cases and so many different places and languages, is sheer nonsense. Nevertheless, the novel as it has generally been written over the past four decades looks markedly different from the novel as it was written in the 1920s, or at the height of the Victorian era, and so the approximations of literary history do point toward empirically observable phenomena, however many exceptions we may be able to pose as objections.

Granted, the international scene of fiction since the Second World War displays many highly divergent trends, including a variety of vigorous survivals of nineteenth-century realism, only slightly modified, if at all, to respond to the pressures of a new historical age. There is, however, a cluster of recurrent features that tends to set off the literature of this period from that of previous eras. The three most salient of these features are a conscious postmodernism, fictional self-reflexivity, and the recourse to fantasy as a means of engaging history. Let me explain each briefly before attempting to see what bearing the whole cluster might have on the first four decades of Hebrew fiction since the establishment of the State of Israel.

The years from the brink of the First World War to the end of the 1920s have come to appear more and more as an extraordinary time of breakthrough achievements in all the arts. R. P. Blackmur once designated the high point of this period, 1921–25, as *anni mirabiles,* the years of wonder, and what else could one call a four-year span that saw the publication of *Ulysses, The Waste Land, The Castle, The Magic Mountain,* four volumes of Proust's masterpiece, and *Mrs. Dalloway?* High modernism continues to manifest itself in notable works beyond the period Blackmur marks as its peak in writers like Broch, Musil, and Faulkner, but it is hardly surprising that since the watershed of the Second World War many novelists have felt the need to measure their own stature against the long shadow cast by the great modernists. Some, unwilling or unable to compete, have turned their backs on the achievement of the modernists, reverting to earlier forms of fiction. The architectonic character of modernist works like *Ulysses* and *A la recherche du temps perdu* has generally been abandoned for a more improvisatory, or at least a more rapidly composed, kind of fiction, but the iconoclasm, both thematic and formal, of the modernists has become a common legacy of novelists in the latter part of the twentieth century. The adversary stance of modernism toward the dominant values of the culture is now often the assumed point of departure for serious writing, and in the case of Israel that is one reason, if only a secondary reason, for the fact that writers constitute a kind of permanent opposition to the political establishment. Technically, much of the energy of modernism was directed toward reshaping the conventions of fiction and breaking the molds of traditional realism. This formal iconoclasm has been abundantly and variously sustained in fiction written since the Second World War, though it is sometimes carried out with a casualness or flippancy that might have surprised the modernists, or with a flaunting of the element of parody that was usually kept subordinate in the great works of the twenties. Similarly, the modernists' acute consciousness of artifice, which to them did not seem incompatible with the aspirations of a renovated realism, has often been pushed to surprising extremes, perhaps most successfully, in opposite ways, by Nabokov and Borges, but also by John Barth, Italo Calvino, Alain Robbe-Grillet, Marguerite Duras, and many others.

The one respect in which the contemporary novel may depart most clearly from its modernist antecedents is in its fondness for fantasy. Among the major writers who flourished in the second and third decades of our century, Kafka alone gives a central role in his work to fantasy, though it is hard to see how the contemporary practitioners of fantasy derive from him except for his having set a general precedent by making a radical break with realism. The writers of our own period who may have some real affinity with Kafka are those, like Borges and Calvino, who use fantasy as a vehicle for the exploration of metaphysical and epistemological puzzles. Such exploration is usually carried out on the miniature scale of the short story. The novel, as in the work of Gabriel García Márquez, Günter Grass, Salman Rushdie, Thomas Pynchon, and Robert Coover, more typically employs fantasy to provide, paradoxically, a coherent vantage on the vertiginous panorama of contemporary history. If World War I, as has so often been observed, was a traumatic watershed in Western history, World War II, unleashing the unspeakable forces of genocide and ending with a weapon capable of destroying mankind, seemed a dread realization of all that had been adumbrated in what was once called the Great War. For writers beyond the European and North American spheres, moreover, the breakup of colonialism after the second war has brought with it a long, bloody aftermath, variously seen as a legacy of colonialism and as a loosing of terrible energies of destruction indigenous to the sundry new nations. Perhaps our endemic sense of global crisis is also reinforced by the new electronic media that insistently make visual, verbal, and auditory images of the many flashpoints of crisis part of our daily consciousness. In any case, some of the most prominent novelists of the postwar era share a feeling that the four-square measure of reason, bound by the laws of nature and probability, is no way to encompass the intrinsic irrationality, the sheer outrageousness, of political-historical reality. And so writers impelled by the keenest urgency of historical seriousness have built their novels around some fantasy assumption: a child who wills himself never to grow beyond the age of three (the confrontation with Nazism in *The Tin Drum*), the gift of perfect telepathy (the confrontation with the murderousness of the Indian subcontinent in *Midnight's Children*), a protagonist who lives for centuries (the confrontation with colonialism and the Latin American mind in *One Hundred Years of Solitude*).

To anyone who has been following developments in the Israeli novel, it should be apparent that this whole schema of contemporary fiction has had very little pertinence, at least for the first two decades of statehood and in most respects not until well into the 1980s. The reasons for the disparity are multiple. To begin with, the antecedents and proximate models of Hebrew fiction have tilted it steeply away from fantasy and self-reflexivity. Modern Hebrew fiction in Europe from its beginnings in the Haskalah was powerfully driven by a need to render a sober account of Jewish society and its problems and even to propose practical means of reform. In this tradition, going back to the 1820s, there was ample room for the didacticism of satire but scant encouragement for the free play of literary artifice. Symptomatically, the new Hebrew prose absorbed the strong influence of Gogol the satirist but very little of Gogol the master of fantasy. There was no Hebrew Sterne or Poe, no Hebrew *Peau de chagrin* or *Dr. Jekyll and Mr. Hyde*. (Both the supernatural and the flaunting of artifice are manifested in the fiction of S. Y. Agnon, from the first decade of our century onward, but Agnon's magisterial achievement, however admired, has not inspired much sustained emulation among the Israeli-bred writers with whom we are concerned.) When the first modern generation of native speakers of Hebrew launched their literary careers in the years just before statehood, the indigenous Hebrew commitment to somber realism was compounded by fealty to an external model. Most of the writers who came of age in the 1940s had grown up in the left-wing youth movements that were central to the *yishuv* (the Zionist settlement) of that period, and a good portion of their early literary nurture was Soviet Socialist Realism in Hebrew translation. One finds figures like the young novelist Moshe Shamir and the young journalist Amos Elon (today, respectively, on the extreme right and the bitterly disaffected left) calling programmatically for a deeply engaged literature that essentially would constitute a Zionist socialist realism. The fiction of the time, though it generally proved less socialist and more disaffected than these young ideologues had hoped, responded to the call of engagement with a morally intent, often drab realism.

Ideology, moreover, was by no means the only motive for realism. There was, quite understandably, an urgent sense of wholly new national realities and an impulse of sheer representation, to get things right in words. What was it like to live in the new social realm of the kibbutz, to struggle with the exhortations and constraints of the youth movement, to be initiated into manhood by the terrible test of arms in the War of Independence, to make one's way through the fifties' changing urban landscape of mass immigration, proliferating bureaucracy, fading idealism, and economic austerity? These relentless challenges of the new Israeli milieux were accompanied by a set of related challenges posed by the Hebrew language. One must keep in mind that this was the first generation of Hebrew writers since antiquity that had imbibed the language naturally as a mother tongue rather than having synthesized it for literary use from a conglomeration of sacred texts, as did Agnon and his contemporaries and predecessors. At least to begin with, the linguistic "naturalness" proved to be something of a mixed blessing. In fiction, considerable energy was directed to fashioning realistic dialogue, complete with phonetic transcriptions of slurred speech and the abundant use of newly minted slang. (When one rereads the fiction of the forties and early fifties today, much of this, because the usage has become obsolete, looks quaint.) Beyond dialogue, the prose of the Generation of 1948 is often literary in a pejorative sense, being a Hebrew reinvention of the clichés of the European novel, not infrequently sprinkled with imperfect imitations of the classicizing style of Agnon, Haim Hazaz, Y. D.

Berkowitz, and other Diaspora-educated writers. This struggle with the inchoate character of the language would continue till the late 1970s, down into the second generation of native Hebrew writers, often disposing novelists to the fundamental effort of realistic representation and providing scant stimulus for the kind of somersaults of the imagination that were being executed in European, North American, and Latin American fiction during these years.

The picture of Israeli prose through the first four decades of statehood is of course an evolving one. The conventional way to chart the changes is with a generational map: the Generation of Forty-eight (Shamir, S. Yizhar, Hanoch Bartov, Natan Shaham), the New Wave that began to publish toward the end of the fifties (Amos Oz, A. B. Yehoshua, Amalia Kahana-Carmon), and the writers of the eighties (David Grossman, Meir Shalev, Ruth Almog, Anton Shammas). This schema has a good deal of explanatory validity but it also illustrates the necessary imprecision of all literary-historical schemata. A generation both is and is not a real entity. Many of the writers of 1948 did rub shoulders, share common experiences, and entertain similar literary aspirations, but there are always writers whose background and sensibility set them apart from their chronological contemporaries. The most striking example in Hebrew prose is offered by Yehuda Amichai, who comes to fiction through poetry. Though his age should make him a member of the Generation of Forty-eight, his surrealist and symbolic narratives have no discernible relation to the fiction of his contemporaries. Or again, Amalia Kahana-Carmon is frequently bracketed by criticism with Yehoshua and Oz, but the deeply personal nature of her enterprise, the eccentricity of her highly wrought prose, her fine attunement to woman's experience, place her at an incalculable tangent to her chronological generation. And of course though writers do sometimes cluster in small groups of likeminded peers close in age, they do not necessarily assemble in neat ranks eighteen years apart, birthdates being just as prone to random distribution as sensibilities and literary projects.

Let me propose another arbitrary map, not to displace the generational one but to complement it by providing a developmental picture of the Israeli novel from a somewhat different angle. For each of the four decades of statehood I shall identify what seems to me the most imposing Hebrew novel (a decade being an obviously mechanical way of defining a unit of historical experience, but hardly more arbitrary than a generation, and free of the misleading biological implications associated with generations). In two of the four cases there would be critical consensus that the novel put forth is the major one of the decade. My other two choices might well invite considerable debate, but I would contend that they are the most original Hebrew novels of their respective decades, though not necessarily the most representative ones. In any case, some brief observations on each of these four way stations of Hebrew fiction should suggest certain lines of evolution in the Israeli novel through its first four decades as well as a shifting pattern of correspondences to fiction written elsewhere. The novels I would like to look at are S. Yizhar's *The Days of Ziklag* (1958, untranslated), Yehuda Amichai's *Not of This Time, Not of This Place* (1964, available in a somewhat abridged English version), Yaakov Shabtai's *Past Continuous* (1977, available in English), and David Grossman's *See Under: Love* (1986, also available in English).

There is no controversy about the commanding place of *The Days of Ziklag* in Hebrew fiction of the fifties. A novel of more than twelve hundred pages, alternating between interior monologues and lengthy dialogues, covering seven days in the battle for a hill in the Negev during the War of Independence, it is clearly the culmination of a whole decade of fiction that struggled to come to terms with the war and all the issues of personal and national identity that the conflict raised for the young fighters. The quality I mentioned earlier of somber intentness in seeking to encompass new historical realities attains its apogee in Yizhar's vast novel. Stylistically, the impulse to fashion a new Israeli literary Hebrew is also pushed as far as it can go, the language heavily loaded with rare or hitherto unused terms as well as with new coinages, the syntax pulled into great sprawling coils for which there is little precedent in previous Hebrew prose. The stress on ethical quandary in a time of crisis owes a good deal to Sartre (this was, of course, the heyday of French existentialism). The luxuriant lyricism of the style and the technical procedures of interior monologue reflect the influence of Faulkner and Thomas Wolfe.

In several respects, *The Days of Ziklag*, which appeared during the flowering of the French New Novel, and just a year before the publication of *The Tin Drum*, betrays a time lag in the relation of the Israeli novel to fiction elsewhere that would persist for another generation. Yizhar's use of a loose approximation of stream of consciousness associates him with the modernist prose of the twenties and thirties. He is, one should note, the only Hebrew novelist of his generation interested in such techniques of interiorization, but this in no way prevents *The Days of Ziklag* from being the exemplary Israeli novel of its decade, as criticism was quick to recognize. For beneath the slow undulations of lyric language, the minutely shaded rendering of states of feeling and perception that subverts a sense of progressive time, stands a sturdy substructure of ideological argumentation. The function of narrativity is qualified and dispersed not so much, as in Faulkner, because the historical world seems to have lost narrative coherence, but rather because the narrative situation is grasped as an occasion for the discussion of political and moral issues. And over against the modernist commitment to the bold exploration of individual experience, Yizhar typifies Israeli fiction of this period in his overriding concern with collective dilemmas and collective destiny: the real protagonist of his novel is not any one character but the peer group.

In its expository or dialectic nature, *The Days of Ziklag* is a novel that speaks resoundingly for a whole generation, and one suspects that behind it is a literary tradition that goes back at least indirectly to nineteenth-century Russia and certainly to Hebrew fiction writers of the early twentieth century like Y. H. Brenner and M. Y. Berdichevsky. What's to be done?, Yizhar's troubled young men under fire ask themselves in interior monologue and tireless discussion. What do we do now, standing at this bloody historical crossroads, with the Diaspora legacy we are supposed to reject, the biblical past we are enjoined to reclaim, the national future our teachers and leaders have led us to imagine as a messianic fulfillment? It is easy to see why such questioning would have deep resonance in the Israeli intelligentsia ten years after independence, though the mode of fiction devised for the questioning was, at least from a comparative perspective, somewhat anachronistic.

Yehuda Amichai's long novel, *Not of This Time, Not of This Place*, seems to me the most original Hebrew work of fiction of the sixties. It is also the first Israeli novel to break decisively with the tacit contract of realism that had been so dutifully observed, and as such it was a harbinger of things to come two decades later. The formally experimental character of *Not of This Time*, its strange mix of the bizarre, the grotesque, and the dreamlike, make it look more like contemporary Western fiction than did any previous Israeli novel, but beyond a motif or two borrowed from Rilke's poetry, foreign influences are hard to detect, and there is surely more Agnon here, however intermittent, than, say, Günter Grass. It is also fair to add that this remarkable book is mainly a poet's work in both its virtues and its flaws. Amichai's primary vocation was, and remains, that of a poet. In the fifties he published a volume of intriguing antirealist stories dense with metaphorical invention and disorienting associative leaps. After *Not of This Time* he would write just one more novel, a much slighter book, in a farcical mode, about an ambivalent Israeli settled in New York. His major work of fiction is a poet's novel in a rigorously definable sense. That is, though the book has a fairly elaborate novelistic apparatus, with a persuasive evocation of social milieu, a complicated cast of characters, and a revelation of destiny through plot, it is a lyric novel because there is finally only one "real" character who, like the speaker of a lyric poem, confronts the quandaries of existence — desire, death, bereavement, memory, evil, love — through reflection and through interaction with a series of shadow images, mirror images, and projections. Even Patricia, the American woman with whom the Israeli protagonist has a consuming affair, proves to be more archetype than individual character — mermaid, Venus, archaic Eve, exotic woman of the wild prairies, a figure alluring and suggestive but an archetype nonetheless.

The chief formal innovation of *Not of This Time* is the splitting of the action into two simultaneous plots that share a single protagonist who in alternating chapters lives out a summer momentously dedicated to love (with Patricia, in Jerusalem, in third-person narration) and to death (in the town where he was born in Germany, in first-person narration, as he tries to touch his own origins and confront the perpetrators of genocide). The two intertwined narratives are linked by an intricate pattern of shared themes and motifs, but their tonalities are quite different. The first-person narrative in Germany is very much the story of a man talking with himself, spooked by nightmarish memory, speaking with people who often seem more than a little like ghosts or hallucinations or sounding boards for his own brooding meditations. The German scenes are manifestly an exploration of the unimaginable, as must be any effort to conceive a supposedly enlightened nation responsible for the carefully planned murder of millions of innocent human beings; perhaps the "meaning" of these chapters is the discovery that the subject, despite the protagonist's illusions to the contrary, is ultimately unimaginable. The Jerusalem narrative, on the other hand, conveys a poignant sense of place and in the story of the love affair vividly enacts the progressive movements of erotic exaltation and obsession. The writer's affection for the zaniness of the Jerusalem scene, its carnivalesque mingling of academic conferences and religious sectarianism, its cityscape of new construction and rubble bisected (in 1964) by barbed wire and no-man's-land, imbues the Jerusalem setting with an appealing liveliness, even as he transforms it into a symbolic resonator of Joel's grand passion for Patricia.

Not of This Time, Not of This Place is a signal achievement but, as I have intimated, not a representative one for the Israeli novel of the sixties. In one respect, however, it would prove to be exemplary. The antirealist device of the two contradictory plots is not, I think, just an ingenious trick but a bending of novelistic convention urged by the pressures of the intolerable subject — an Israeli, child of European Jewry, trying to sort out the predictable confusions of feeling and value of his adult life against the abysmal background of the Holocaust that cannot be expunged from memory. What occurred between 1933 and 1945 is such a radical violation of all the coordinates of quotidian reality we have lived with since that some kind of fracturing of the logical consistencies of realism seems required to imagine in one verbal structure existence then and now. In Amichai's novel, the disparity between the two realms is above all focused in the thematic opposition between two different orientations toward time. The third-person Joel is wholly absorbed in the present tense of passionate consummation, the "now" he cries out at the moment of sexual climax. The first-person Joel, attempting in Germany to pursue his vocation of archeologist in a sphere of moral history, is obsessed with memory, and discovers that the past he tries to dig up is bottomless. The bifurcated structure of Amichai's novel is of course not something another novelist would want to imitate directly, but the book does suggest that the attempt to encompass the landscape of genocide in fiction might be carried out most persuasively by moving beyond the commonsensical confines of realist convention.

If in the mid-sixties the gap between innovations in Hebrew fiction and fiction elsewhere could be closed only by the idiosyncrasy of a poet's novel, the Israeli novel since the late seventies has moved toward the international forefront in a remarkable stream of convincingly original works. Among these I would include Amos Oz's *A Perfect Peace* (1982) and A. B. Yehoshua's *Molkho* (1987; in English, *Five Seasons*), two very different novels of mature psychological realism by the leading New Wave writers who began in more symbolic modes; Aharon Appelfeld's quietly phantasmagoric *Badenheim 1939* (1979); Meir Shalev's enchanting mixture of historical realism and droll or grotesque fantasy, a kind of Hebrew *Hundred Years of Solitude*, ironically called *A Russian Novel* (1988, retitled *The Blue Mountain* in its English version); Anton Shammas's engaging if uneven *Arabesques* (1986); and David Grossman's 1986 novel, *See Under: Love*, which we shall consider presently. But the real turning point in the coming of age of the Hebrew novel was the publication in 1977 of Yaakov Shabtai's *Past Continuous*. In Israel there is a solid critical consensus that nothing else in this decade equals the originality of Shabtai's achievement. (Because our concern is with writers who grew up in Israel, Agnon's posthumous *Shira*, 1971, is excluded from consideration.) Precisely because of the boldness of its formal innovations, which I will try to describe briefly, *Past Continuous* has had no imitators. Stylistically, however, it is a brilliant solution to the problems of language with which Hebrew writers had been struggling since the 1940s. (Amichai's novel could not offer a general model for confronting this problematic of style because it is in many respects a transposition into prose of the stylistic habits of his poetry and thus bears his signature as a personal solution.) The prose of the Generation of 1948 was often overwrought, and a flamboyant version of that fault is detectable in the early Amos Oz, while the early Yehoshua reacts to his predecessors by working in a drab, deliberately circumscribed stylistic register. Shabtai succeeded in creating a supple new synthesis, fashioning a narrative language that was deeply and naturally rooted in colloquial usage while it utilized the lexical range and the power of fine discrimination of the literary Hebrew that had been perfected in successive stages from the 1880s onward. Although the claim I shall make may be hard to substantiate because no other writer sounds very much like Shabtai, I would contend that the new subtlety and unstrained stylistic richness one encounters in Hebrew prose of the last decade (Grossman, Shalev, the later Yehoshua) owes a good deal, at least indirectly, to the powerful precedent of usage set by Shabtai.

Past Continuous gives the distinct impression of a gifted novelist working out in literary form the sinuous course of his personal vision without much consciousness of models, whether foreign or indigenous. The result, in any case, is more a modernist than a contemporary project, more like Proust, Joyce, Musil, or Faulkner than, say, Butor or Cortázar. The novel's formal innovations are rigorous and uncompromising, without much sense of easy free play or self-reflexivity; stylistic, typographical, and narrative conventions are strenuously redefined in the service of a hyperrealism. Although the word "continuous" does not actually appear in the original Hebrew title, the idea is manifest in the very typography, which confronts the reader with 275 pages uninterrupted by a single paragraph break, chapter division, or any other form of spacing (this feature was not retained in the English version). There are punctuated sentences, but they typi-

cally wind their way across half a page or a page of type, so that sometimes one almost loses track of the beginning by the end. This stretching of syntax into elaborate elastic convolutions makes it an apt
vehicle for Shabtai's hyperrealism. Nothing is discrete or neatly seg-
mented in his world. Again and again, different persons, places, and
times are caught up together in a single web. We live, Shabtai assumes,
in the most complicating connexity, and so he devises sentences —
which in turn produce a slow narrative undulation instead of linear
narration — that loop back and forth through different characters and
different moments, in montages made up of reported feelings and ac-
tions, analysis of motives, transcriptions of thought, dialogue, and indications of scene. It is as though all the narrative functions of the traditional realist novel had been broken into very small pieces and then
spun together in a centrifuge somehow programmed to give them a
new purposeful design. In this way, *Past Continuous* manages to provide a minute and persuasive account of both social and psychological
realities: the extended family (still a more potent presence in Israel
than in most other modern states), the network of friends and lovers,
the interplay of politics and society, the fluidity of consciousness, and,
arching over everything in Shabtai's somber vision, the terrible twin
forces of death and decay. It is with *Past Continuous*, as I have intimated, that the Israeli novel, somewhat surprisingly, joins the van-
guard of postwar fiction. It is a book easily as radical as any French
New Novel in the recasting of the conventions of fiction, but at the
same time informed by existential urgency, without a sense of formal
experiment carried out for its own sake, or to achieve literary self-def-
inition in relation to one's fictional forebears. Shabtai's death at the
age of forty-seven, just four years after the appearance of *Past Continuous*, was an incalculable loss to Hebrew literature, but the legacy of
his stylistic synthesis is likely to be a lasting resource for Hebrew
writers.

   After Shabtai, in the eighties, postmodernism makes a dramatic en-
trance on the Israeli literary scene. Three recent novels that have already been mentioned — *Arabesques, A Russian Novel*, and *See Under: Love* — exhibit in varying manners and degrees the contemporary

fondness for fantasy, parody, playfulness, and flaunted awareness of the artifices of fiction. David Grossman's novel is the most ambitious and, in my view, the most compelling of the three, and I think it evinces an order of originality that will continue to loom over other Hebrew fiction of the decade. Let me describe its peculiar four-part structure, the range of its stylistic strategies, and how these relate to the book's troubling thematic concerns.

See Under: Love is a novel about the Holocaust, or more precisely, about the inescapable need and the necessary incapacity of the imagination to comprehend the Holocaust. As in the case of Amichai, a fundamental break with the conventions of realism is made in order to get at the sheer impossibility of the subject, though Grossman's antirealism is more formally complicated and more extreme. The novel comprises four long chapters, each written in a very different style and a very different narrative mode. The first section is the only one that adheres to the norms of realism, and I should add that it is also the only section that has elicited enthusiasm even from Hebrew readers otherwise hostile to the book. (In Israel, the novel was a spectacular bestseller, with criticism sharply divided over its merits.) Narrated in the third person from the point of view of a nine-year-old boy growing up in Jerusalem in the late fifties, this section is indeed one of the most remarkable recreations of a child's sense of the world in recent fiction anywhere. The boy, Momik, is the child of concentration camp survivors, living in a community that seems composed almost exclusively of other survivors. The world, then, that he tries to understand has a kind of black hole of history at its core, of which Momik learns through hints and whispers and conversations abruptly cut off when he enters the presence of the adults. What they don't want to tell him about is what really happened "there," and so he creates an elaborate fantasy about the Land of There, compounded of misconstrued tag ends of information and things he has read in children's adventure stories. Even the tattooed numbers on the arms of the survivors are part of Momik's desperate game: he tries to memorize them so that he can decipher the conspiratorial code he is sure they contain.

The ground for the remaining three parts of the novel is prepared by the sudden appearance in Momik's world of a babbling old man, presumed to be his grandfather, Anshel Wasserman, who in Europe was a writer of Hebrew children's fiction during the teens and twenties, and who has been utterly broken by his experience in the camps, reduced to reciting an endless litany of four words: "Herr Neigel Nazi kaput." The last three sections are all the inventions of the adult Momik, who has become a writer (as well as, in a troubled way, a husband and father) consumed by the obsession of trying to imagine what Grandpa Anshel underwent in the *anus mundi*. The second section, "Bruno," is a mythic counter-version of the death of the Polish-Jewish writer Bruno Schulz, who in fact was shot by a Nazi officer in the ghetto of Drohobych in 1942. Momik's Bruno escapes to Danzig, where he jumps off a wharf with the intention of committing suicide. Instead, he metamorphoses by stages into a salmon, joining a school of salmon that swims round the globe and leads him beyond any human sense of self into the primordial fierceness of aqueous life. This section is written in an elaborately lyric prose reminiscent of Schulz's own style, and perhaps also owing something to Yizhar's Hebrew, counterpointed by monologues of the Sea—here a female mythic figure—speaking to Momik in pungent colloquial Hebrew. Language itself is very much at issue in this chapter, and to a large degree in the last two chapters as well. Can art, the novel asks, create an explosively new, revelatory, "messianic" language, as the historical Bruno Schulz dreamed, or is all human speech doomed to obscenity once it has made it possible for one Nazi officer to say in German to another in the Drohobych ghetto, "You killed my Jew, now I'm going to kill your Jew"?

The third and fourth sections are the story of Anshel Wasserman and of his tormentor/*semblable*, the camp commandant, Herr Neigel. Wasserman, it emerges, has been gifted or blighted with an embarrassing inability to die. A Luger fired at his temple produces no more than an odd buzzing in his ears while the bullet goes whizzing into the woodwork. Wasserman, who has seen his only daughter murdered before his eyes, by Neigel, and his wife marched off to the gas chambers, wants nothing but death. When it becomes clear that the Nazi commandant in his childhood was an avid reader of Wasserman's naively idealistic adventure stories in German translation (something of an improbability, it must be admitted), the two hit upon an anti-Scheherazade pact: each night Wasserman will read to Neigel a new installment of his stories featuring the old heroes (he actually recites from a blank notebook), and as a reward, each night, at the end of the reading, Neigel will try again to kill him. What happens is that a weird complicity is woven between the two men, with Neigel in the end becoming a kind of literary collaborator of his Jewish prisoner. Through the instrument of literature, Wasserman works a crack in the psychological armor of the mass murderer, touches his humanity (for even the ideological killer has a wife and children and a remnant of naive aspirations), finally destroying him through the power of the story. The last chapter, which concludes this plot, is entitled "The Complete Encyclopedia of the Life of Kazik." Kazik, a miracle-baby born in Wasserman's story, lives the whole cycle of human life in a twenty-four-hour span. The narrative of his life, which is intertwined with the story of Wasserman and Neigel who invent it, is arranged as a series of encyclopedia entries in alphabetic order, from 'aleph, 'ahavah, "love," to tav, tefilah, "prayer."

Although there is hardly space in my rapid survey to account for this whole complex intermesh of bizarre invention and modes of narration, a few words about the styles of *See Under: Love* and the force of its self-reflexivity may suggest where it stands in both the evolution of the Israeli novel and on the contemporary international scene. Grossman's extraordinarily resourceful experiment with styles presupposes the assurance of linguistic achievement before him— presupposes, I would say, Shabtai and Yizhar and the solidification of Hebrew usage in the sundry spheres of daily life, as well as the rich abundance of Hebrew translations of European and American fiction. The novel ranges from children's language ("Momik") to a poet's language ("Bruno") to the detached, passive-voiced prose of an encyclopedia, with insets of the quaintly ornate, old-fashioned European Hebrew of Wasserman, the middle literary diction of the adult Momik as narrator, the racy colloquialism of the Sea, and the educated Israeli

Hebrew of Neigel, who is of course actually speaking German. This spectrum of styles reflects the urgency that drives the novel's self-reflexive mode. How do you construct a story, using language, to tell about events that make mockery of narrative's sense-seeking impulse? The child Momik, with his "spy notebook" in which he tries to record his understanding of the Land of There, adumbrates the impossible predicament of the adult writer. The rest of the novel then becomes a series of Chinese-box structures of fictional self-consciousness: the adult Momik inventing his "Bruno," who is a reflection and transmutation of the life and prose of the writer Bruno Schulz; again, the adult Momik writing about Wasserman, who "writes" at the heart of historical darkness about his old heroes struggling with a ghastly new reality; and, finally, Momik the writer merging with the anonymous "editors" responsible for the "Encyclopedia" that tells of Wasserman and his characters without ever ceasing to address Momik and his predicament as he looks back at the Holocaust a generation later. In this narrative hall of mirrors, it is Neigel, the dutiful bureaucrat of genocide, who complains, "I like simple stories"; to which Wasserman, here a spokesman for the author, rejoins, "There are no longer simple stories." For some readers, both in Israel and elsewhere, this whole elaborate structure is too clever by half for representing its ghastly subject. It is, I would concede, the kind of writing that runs risks (and at least in the "Bruno" section may lead to excesses), but it also has the power to illuminate recent history in unexpected ways.

Grossman shares with writers like Grass, García Márquez, and Rushdie a sense that the laws of nature may have to be abrogated by the novelist in order to body forth in fiction the appalling murderousness of twentieth-century reality. The wealth of attention he devotes to language and the artifices of fiction is also very contemporary, but at the same time it might well be but a new mode of the historical and existential seriousness that has characterized Hebrew literary tradition before him. For this distinctively Hebrew version of self-reflexive fiction raises questions we can scarcely avoid asking, again and again: four decades after a civilized nation was finally interrupted only by force from its manic task of translating all of European Jewry into smoke, how can we make sense of humanity in history, how then can any tale be told, how can we find a truly human language?

7/ VISTAS OF ANNIHILATION

The murder of more than a third of the Jewish people in six years of unspeakable horror continues to impose a disturbing dilemma on the kinds of political, intellectual, or spiritual lives Jews try to make for themselves as Jews. To turn their gaze from these events is to ignore the abysmal potential of the realm of history in which the Jewish people and humanity at large are, perforce, profoundly involved. But to ponder the vistas of annihilation too much may lead, as I once had occasion to argue,* to a kind of pornography of horror that distorts one's vision of what Jews have been or might become and that, in both academic life and in the popular media, has already produced a veritable Holocaust industry.

Perhaps some of the deplorable consequences of excessive concentration on the Holocaust have stemmed from the strong tendency to define it as an awesomely unique event in Jewish history. I hardly want to deny that in Hitler's war against the Jews genocide reached an order of magnitude, and ideologically grounded evil attained a systematic pervasiveness, that have no equals in the previous experience of the Jewish people. But to insist, as so many have, on the imperative uniqueness of the event is to encourage seeing it in a vacuum, thus reducing all the variegated stuff of Jewish history to a prelude to the gas chambers.

* "Deformations of the Holocaust," *Commentary,* February 1981.

The ghettos of Warsaw and Lodz, which have lately been receiving renewed attention, were not symbolic theaters of destruction set against the backdrop of eternity, but dense intersections of all the richly contradictory forces that made up modern Polish Jewry — Bundism, Zionism, Hebraism, Yiddishism, assimilation, Hasidism, neo-Orthodoxy — together with the variously selective memories and forgettings of antecedent Jewish experience that each of these groups fostered. The Jews brought with them to the arenas of destruction all their sundry internal divisions, their individual and collective defects, and, one must surely add, their various inner resources, whether recently acquired or developed over the centuries. An awareness of such continuities and such complicating backgrounds may make it possible to see that, however traumatic the Hitler years were, Jewish history neither ended nor began with them.

Given this urgent need to set the Holocaust in a larger context, two new books on Jewish literary responses to historical disaster are particularly welcome corrections to critical discussions that have tended to represent the world exclusively in ghastly black-and-white photos illuminated by the baleful light of the crematoria. *Hurban* and *Against the Apocalypse* are clearly conceived as coordinate studies. The respective authors, Alan Mintz and David Roskies, are close friends and fellow editors of a new academic quarterly, *Prooftexts: A Journal of Jewish Literary History*. Both books use the phrase "responses to catastrophe" in their subtitles, and in his preface Mintz indicates that he and Roskies have divided up the territory, he concentrating entirely on Hebrew materials and Roskies chiefly on Yiddish. There are certain differences in tone, historical scope, and critical strategy between the two books, though both deserve praise for their lucidity, their carefully made critical distinctions, and the balanced historical perspective in which they place their subjects.

Mintz focuses his argument through critical readings of a limited number of major texts, beginning with Lamentations and then moving rapidly through Midrash to the Middle Ages, but concentrating on modern works by Mendele Mokher Seforim, Haim Nachman Bialik, Shaul Tchernichovsky, Uri Zvi Greenberg, Aharon Appelfeld, and Dan

Pagis. Roskies begins his main story with the reactions in Yiddish literature to the pogroms of 1881 and advances by stages through the sundry disasters of the earlier twentieth century to the Holocaust, offering a more panoramically detailed overview than does Mintz. Both share the conviction, which they succeed in making persuasive, that there exists not an absolute catastrophe, 1939–45, but a complicated history of responses to catastrophe, in some ways continuous, in others composed of certain radical departures, and this history enters significantly into the effort of most Hebrew and Yiddish writers to apprehend imaginatively the latest and worst of the disasters. In both cases, the discussions of premodern texts are less compelling than the investigations of materials written in the last hundred years, but one sees why the larger historical frame of reference was important for both writers.

The centerpiece of Mintz's book is the series of astute interpretations and evaluations he offers of poems by Tchernichovsky ("Baruch of Mainz"), Bialik ("In the City of Slaughter"), and Greenberg (*Streets of the River*), and of short fiction by Appelfeld. In all these readings, he is attentive to formal issues like style, poetic or narrative form, imagery, and genre, but he keeps steadily in view the question of how the deployment of these formal elements may be judged as an adequate or authentic response to the historical predicament addressed by the writer. In other words, though Mintz sometimes conjures with current critical terms such as the metaphor-metonymy opposition made popular by Roman Jakobson, his underlying concept of the task of criticism goes back to Lionel Trilling and other New York critics of the forties and fifties.

Roskies's initially puzzling title has a double meaning: some of the writers he considers — perhaps most notably, the great Yiddish poet, Avraham Sutzkever — have used their work to resist an apocalyptic understanding of the terrible events; more generally, Roskies's own decision to recoup a historical tradition implies a refusal of the apocalyptic perspective:

The Jewish people are at the point of ... allowing the Holocaust to become the crucible of their culture. I have set out to challenge the validity of this apocalyptic tendency by arguing for the vitality of Jewish response to catastrophe, never as great as in the last hundred years. And responses to the Holocaust do not mark the end of the process.

Of course, it is not easy to say what precisely might constitute "vitality" in an activity so grim as literary responses to mass murder. I would like to propose and illustrate one direction in which an answer might lie, but in order to do that I want first to stress an important assumption about what the imagination makes of catastrophe that is suggested in somewhat different terms by both Roskies and Mintz. As these overviews of Yiddish and Hebrew literary history reveal, there is an inescapable conservative bias built into literary expression. To respond to a set of historical circumstances, however radically disturbing, through a poem or a story or a play, is to invoke your own consciousness of a whole literary corpus with its conventions and norms, and of any number of individual poems, stories, or plays. Even the aggressive iconoclast somehow uses the images he shatters and scrambles, so that all literature proves to be in some way a superimposition of the past on the present. An especially instructive instance of this phenomenon is the powerful presence in the Warsaw ghetto, documented by Roskies, of Bialik's 1903 poem on the Kishinev pogrom, "Upon the Slaughter." Yitzhak Katzenelson, the leading Yiddish poet of the ghetto, could go so far as to say, "Thanks to Bialik, our most profound [experiences] have been given eternal form and this has lifted a great burden from us."

This formal conservatism of literary expression raises questions about the adequacy of literary response to the disruptive and shifting movements of historical experience. The obvious advantage of such conservatism is that we preserve in acute adversity a sustaining sense of continuity with what we have been before, drawing on sets of images, systems of explanation, even the tonal nuances of particular words and idioms, inherited from the past. The fundamental disadvantage is that the redeployment of all these inherited resources may lead us to lie about the present or at least to misapprehend in some way its terrible differentness. Literature ineluctably works with what Roskies calls "archetypes" and what Mintz calls "paradigms," which by their generalizing character may go too far in harmonizing present experience with past assumptions.

The problem of such schematization, however is more pervasive in ritual and the various shorthands of collective memory than it is in individual literary expression. Roskies, commenting on the memorial plaques for the destroyed towns of Lithuania that have been placed in the Choral Synagogue of Vilna, observes: "When Jews now mourn in public, . . . they preserve the collective memory of the collective disaster, but in so doing fall back on symbolic constructs and ritual acts that necessarily blur the specificity and the implacable contradictions of the event." Mintz makes a similar remark about the way Jewish historiography and liturgy tend to reduce disasters to a chain of dates and place names ("Auschwitz" as a designation for the entire Holocaust): "In Jewish history the serial linkage of paradigmatic years and places makes a clear statement about the way in which discrete historical catastrophes are drained of their discreteness and absorbed into a larger tradition."

The literary imagination, I would argue, has the possibility of transcending this dilemma because it does not merely use inherited symbolic constructs but constantly disturbs them — and the activity of disturbance has become the more prominent with the emergence of literary modernism. (In Hebrew and Yiddish, modernist tensions become visible after 1881; the process in Hebrew begins in prose with Mendele's vehemently ironic allusivity and takes another two decades to begin to surface — thematically, though not yet formally — in poetry with Bialik and Tchernichovsky.) There is, of course, a broad spectrum of varying literary responses to catastrophe that many readers will feel to be valid, but most of the texts discussed by Roskies and Mintz, whatever the styles and rhetorical strategies of the writers, in some way swerve from the neatness of inherited archetypes, and use literary language to resist the foreclosure of meanings encouraged by ritual, theology, ideology, and the sheer laziness of popular consciousness.

Mintz, at the end of the survey of Israeli literature about the Holocaust with which he concludes his study, spells out this underlying principle: "Literary art has succeeded in stimulating a deeper encounter with the event and thereby put a brake on its premature absorption into a preexisting framework of meaning." What Mintz has in mind specifically in referring to premature absorption is the tendency within Israeli culture to make political capital out of the Holocaust, but his generalization holds for many of the major texts of Hebrew and Yiddish literature of the past hundred years. My one small reservation concerns the phrase, "a deeper encounter with the event." Literature leaves us, willy-nilly, with an elaborate verbal mediation of any historical event, and for this particular event, those of us lucky enough to have been born in another place or time have reason to be grateful that we did not and cannot "encounter" it. What we should not avoid confronting is the idea – or rather, the many competing ideas – of the event, the multiple reverberations it continues to send through our collective and individual lives. In precisely this regard, the varied imaginative responses of literature can be salutary by enabling us as readers to make the precarious yet indispensable effort to effect some alignment between the event and the symbolic constructs of the Jewish past. It is here, I think, that the "vitality" of response of which Roskies speaks is chiefly to be found.

Generalizations about a process like this, which depends on the specificity of the individual literary text, will not be very meaningful, and so I would like to illustrate the principle through three very different poems by Israeli poets. The texts I have chosen all relate, but only obliquely, to the horror of the Holocaust. I of course do not mean to imply that this is the only valid way to write about the subject, but obliqueness does have its advantages – because it avoids the sadomasochistic excesses of sensationalism and because for the most part the Holocaust now persists in our experience through aftershocks of consciousness and indirect effects on our inner lives and our collective existence. As it happens, two of the three poems I will translate (none of them is discussed by Mintz) are by writers who are not at all thought of as important Israeli poets. Malachi Beit-Arié is an archival librarian who has also published poetry; Shulamith Hareven is better known as a novelist. The third poem is by the leading Hebrew poet, Yehuda Amichai. Of the three, only Beit-Arié is a native Israeli, Amichai and Hareven having been brought as children to Palestine, from Germany and Poland respectively, as the Holocaust began to unfold.

Beit-Arié's poem is called "Between Flesh." The title in Hebrew makes an untranslatable pun essential to the meaning of the whole, since *beyn besarim*, between flesh, pointedly echoes *ha-brit beyn habetarim*, the Covenant between the Cleft Animal Parts recorded in Genesis 15. The poem:

> Your velvet nakedness, in this gloom,
> there is no God, you. All me, all you.
> The blood's high tide,
> The fragrance of the flesh.
>
> And behold a great dark dread descends
> in this gloom, your flesh in my eyes,
> in one smoking day was cleft,
> flesh
> and blood,
> in this gloom, your velvet nakedness
> your flesh – and theirs.

This is a strangely exalted erotic poem, the exaltation deriving in large part from the abundant verbal and imagistic recollections of the covenant between Abraham and God. That formative event of Israelite history takes place in the "gloom" (the unusual word *'alatah*, used twice here) of nightfall, Abraham sunk into a trance, sitting on one side of the cut animal pieces and God on the other. The first line of the second stanza here reproduces integrally the last clause of Gen. 15:12, and the "smoking oven [or brazier] and flaming torch" that mysteriously pass between the pieces in the biblical story are alluded to in the telescoped phrase, "one smoking day." Most daringly, the cleft parts of Genesis are transformed in the poem into the cleft flesh (the same verbal stem, *b-t-r*) of the naked female body.

It would seem, then, that the sexual encounter has radically displaced the covenantal one. The lover affirms his purely human sense of solemn connection, experiencing, in the exaltation of carnal consummation, Abraham's fear and trembling. There is no God in this ecstatic moment, everything being absorbed in the "all" of the man speaking and of the woman addressed, the very linkage of the biblical idiom "flesh-and-blood" broken down to the imperious immediacy of its physical components: blood, flesh. The mystery of the scene in Genesis suffuses the poem, but it has become, most urgently, the mystery of carnality.

The poem, however, is more disorienting than I have so far suggested, for its very last word opens up a vertiginous new horizon of signification. Who are the "they" whose flesh so uncannily interrupts the absolute twoness of erotic intimacy? The last two words in the Hebrew are literally "your-flesh – their-flesh" (*besareikh-besaram*), so the meaning of the poem turns on the referent of a final possessive suffix. It is unlikely that it could refer to the flesh of the slaughtered animals in Genesis 15 because the inert creatures have no vital presence in the biblical story and are never designated in it as flesh; the poem's transformation, moreover, of cloven animal parts into woman's flesh would become confused by a suggestion at the end that the biblical *betarim* (animal parts) were also *besarim* (human flesh). A dedicatory note in the original publication of the poem indicates that the poet had clearly in mind a moment of historical violence that impinges directly upon all Israelis – the loss of friends in fighting against the Arabs. But, as is so often the case in literary expression, the choice of language is, I think, overdetermined, and what emerges is a kind of multiple superimposition of images: the erotic encounter, then the consciously chosen image of wartime death in the desert, and then, through the associative momentum of the language, a still grimmer scene of death, in another place. In the terrific compactness of the poem, the smoking day, the descending darkness, the recollection of the word "oven" (which appears along with "smoking" in Genesis 15 though not in the poem), and the heavy stress on blood and flesh lead inexorably back to the landscape of the death camps where murdered millions were shoveled into the flames in an awful reversal of God's promise to Abraham (Gen. 15:5) that his seed would be multitudinous as the stars. A very different prospect of meaning for "there is no God" now comes into view.

Psychologically, the poem records the flickering intervention of a nightmare image in a moment of ecstasy. The woman's lovely nakedness, so rapturously evoked by the lover, triggers a recollection, associatively mediated by the images drawn from Genesis 15, of naked bodies in the crematoria. The disturbance of archetypes in the poem makes it a very private text with strong public reverberations. Not all of us may be visited by the particular nightmare hinted in the poem's last word, but this astonishing fusion of disjunct realms intimates how, as a fact of consciousness after the Holocaust, the shadow of horror can at any moment pass over the heart of joy, and, simultaneously, how the supposed heirs of covenantal assurances may find themselves lost in the wilderness of a history without God.

In contrast to the passionate intensity of "Between Flesh," Shulamith Hareven's "Noah in the Regions of the Sea" seems relaxed, engagingly satiric, even jocular. This difference in tone is possible because the poet is dealing not with the irruption of an image of the horror into the present but with a survivor's difficulties in coping with the quotidian reality that is the aftermath of catastrophe:

> Noah, skinny as a well-crane,
> still with his flood-legs,
> goes tottering through the sunset
> like a walking sail, and hears
> the crunching of his neighbors' bones
> in the vast sand, *tzakh-tzakh.*
>
> The gentle waters
> brought him coppery light, and a buoy,
> and his reflection
> which is never clear.
>
> His feet flounder through the sand
> and the salt earth, patiently. His love
> is doomed to be temporary.

As yet he has no fixed address.

Noah is learning a new language,
learning lone and stone and bow.
Since landing, he's grown a mustache,
signed for his Agency bed and two blankets,
is still not used to the thorns
and doesn't understand his dreams, as though
there were a mistake, no dream, not his.

Maybe the next wave will wipe out
everything, pain and ruined mouth, for
childhood doesn't grow, no never,
it covers up in layers like a thickening conch.

Noah walks between seasons,
through the mother-of-pearl and the skeletons.
Were he questioned, he'd repeat the question
with startled concentration. In the sand
the language of answers is crunched, *tzakh-tzakh.*

Noah goes off. He's getting used to things,
only the mosquitoes. As to the matter of lightning,
he's been assured it is over.

The persistent presence of allusions to the Bible in even the most
colloquial or avant-garde Hebrew poetry has often been remarked. In
many instances, such allusions have been crucial in poems responding
to the Holocaust because through allusion an imaginative confrontation is effected between the symbolic instruments used by tradition to
define meaning and the event that seems a disruption of all meaning.
In the premodern period, Hebrew poets facing catastrophe sought in
one way or another to harmonize their awareness of the biblical background with their perception of the grim historical foreground. In our
own century, beginning strikingly with Bialik's Kishinev poems, poetry has become a theater of antagonism between classical text and
contemporary trauma. In such antagonism there is no simple winner:
for the most part, the biblical text is not flatly rejected but rather
tested, shaken, unsettled, and wrenched into a new orientation.

That process works equally but differently in "Between Flesh" and "Noah in the Regions of the Sea." In the former, the biblical past eerily invades the present; in the latter, a moment of the biblical story is entirely reconstructed in the image of the present. For this reason, allusion in the Hareven poem is solely to the narrative situation in Genesis, not to its language or images (the only distinctive term from the biblical Noah story in the entire poem is "bow" at the beginning of the fourth stanza). Obviously but effectively, Noah here has been recast as a survivor of the European catastrophe who has arrived in Israel, been given his new immigrant's basic equipment by the Jewish Agency, and who can't get used to the mosquitoes – or to a world where everyone he knew is dead. Disproportion, incongruity, and grotesqueness are prominent in this portrait of Noah floundering through the sand and crushed bones, skinny as a well-crane, like a walking sail, for the poem enacts an experience of total disorientation of a man who finds himself, after the cataclysm, cast up, virtually alone, on the shore of an unfamiliar world.

In what way is this reshaping of the Noah story more than just a clever literary trick? In one respect, the poem might be thought of as a kind of midrashic fleshing-out of the biblical story, showing in contemporary terms what it must have been like for Noah to begin life again after the whole world he had known was wiped out. The Deluge in Genesis, as the story of divine wrath against humanity that destroys all but a tiny handful of survivors, may be a plausible emblem for the Holocaust, but if it begins with God's anger, it ends with His covenantal promise to Noah never again to devastate the earth with a flood. In "Noah in the Regions of the Sea," God is absent either as the agent of destruction or as the guarantor of the future. Indeed, even Noah's family, the nucleus of biological regeneration, is absent, so that he is alone with his neighbors' bones and the ambiguous language of the crunching sand. The only hint of other human presences is the bureaucracy that has given him his bed and blankets and that, in its characteristically impersonal language ("As to the matter of lightning"), promises him that the Deluge will not come again. This is a kind of assurance utterly different from God's ringing and repeated promise to Noah (Gen. 8:21–22; 9:11–17) that there will be no second cataclysm – different not only in its impersonality but in its evasive vagueness, which leads us to suspect it may be worth no more than any other bureaucratic promise.

The archetypal background of the biblical Deluge story makes this contemporary Noah not just a special case of survivor but a sort of Jewish Everyman after the Holocaust. At the same time, a principal theme of the original archetype has been unsettled, because the new Noah must begin again uneasily, pondering the vanished world from which he came, wondering what havoc the next wave will wreak, clinging to a tenuous promise of futurity. There are, of course, many other possible constructions of the Jewish condition after 1945, but "Noah in the Regions of the Sea," in so vividly embodying the outward uncertainties and inner bafflement of the survivor who nevertheless strives to go on, illustrates the nuanced effectiveness of poetry as a response to collective disaster.

My final illustration, a poem from Yehuda Amichai's volume *The Hour of Grace* (1982), evokes a postwar setting – one assumes, in Germany – without any recourse to biblical allusion. The poem is called "The Inn of the Sun":

> The Inn of the Sun in the mountains. We stayed there
> a day or two. People talked by great windows
> toward the darkness.
> The high grass wanted us to cry
> and in the hazy valley elegant tennis players
> silently played, as if with no ball.
> And the sad-eyed ones came to the clear-voiced ones
> and said: you are living in my house that was
> my house. A big tree grew here. What did you do to it?
>
> The Inn of the Sun. We stayed there
> two or three days.
> And in the white rooms remembrance and hope,
> night and eternal salvation
> for those who will never return,
> the pallor of death on the great curtains
> and a golden giggle behind the walls.

Planes passed overhead
and above them a camouflage net made of stars
so we won't see no God is there.

But below, at the heavy table
Amid the smoke and alcohol fumes,
a heavy Christian and a light Jew
work together on a new faith.

The Inn of the Sun. "A light rain then fell."
That's all that remains of the Inn of the Sun.

The poem is in several ways uncharacteristic of Amichai. The displacement of his usual emphatically personal first-person singular by the unspecified first-person plural, the use of fragmentary narrative, the vaguely located Central European setting are oddly (if inadvertently) reminiscent of the fiction of Aharon Appelfeld. The poem is a kind of ghost story, and most of its details are quietly orchestrated to produce the appropriate ghostly effects. The Inn of the Sun, one gathers, is a gracious, old-fashioned European mountain resort recalling the prewar era, with great curtained windows looking out on the mountain landscape and on the tennis courts in the valley below. But the lighting is arranged so that everything in the scene dissolves into shadows and fog. The guests at the windows seem to be speaking, in the oddness of the syntax, not to each other but "toward the darkness." There is haze in the valley where the tennis players, eerily, play "as if with no ball." The heavy table stands in a cloud of smoke and alcohol fumes, the curtains glimmer with a deathly pallor, and the only indications of brightness are in the disquieting "golden giggle" behind the walls and in the mere name of the Inn of the Sun, which is actually swathed in night.

Coordinated with this play of darkness, haze, and smoke is a blurring of temporal indications. The stay at the inn is a day or two, then two or three; the suggestion of a scene at nightfall or perhaps late afternoon in the first stanza is succeeded by an intimation of things occurring, not necessarily sequentially, late at night in the rest of the poem. At the end, the recollection dissolves in a remembered remark about rain, like some evanescent hallucination melting in the sea of real time.

What is also noteworthy, especially if one considers that Amichai is a poet who depends a great deal on the brilliance, even the extravagance, of his inventive use of metaphor, is the muted quality of figurative language in the poem. Apart from the personification of the grass in the first stanza (where the otherwise buried pathos of the speaker surfaces) and the epithet "golden" attached to "giggle," the poem is devoid of clearly figurative language – with the exception of the camouflage net made of stars at the end of the second stanza. This is the kind of metaphor, which juxtaposes contemporary military reality with a religious or metaphysical realm, that Amichai has made one of his poetic trademarks. Here it is reserved for the thematic climax, while in the rest of the poem the supernatural character of spectral presences is conveyed in a series of literal utterances, as though what is eerie might have become merely melodramatic by too much metaphorical elaboration.

The words of the sad-eyed ones – obviously, the specters of the murdered or banished Jews – to those who have displaced them seem deliberately chosen for their simple predictability, and turn on an expressive redundancy, "you are living in my house that was / my house," as if through repetition the speakers were trying to assimilate the stubborn fact that remains unassimilable. In any case, the sense of spectral flickering and dissolution that pervades the poem is a perfectly apt correlative for an ex-European Jew's perception of Europe one generation after: a world has vanished as though it never were, but the memory, real and fantasized, of those who once inhabited that world floats back over it, still trying to take in the actuality of irrevocable uprooting.

I noted earlier that Jewish literary responses to modern historical disaster are made up of both continuities with the past and radical breaks from it. Perhaps one may see that most clearly in the changing absences of God in our three poems. I suspect that when a Jew writes a poem about the Holocaust, at least if he or she is writing in Hebrew or Yiddish, it is hard to avoid making God in some way an issue, how-ever implicitly. (This is true even of a poet with so thoroughly secular a perspective as Dan Pagis.) The speaker in "Between Flesh" intransi-gently declares "There is no God" – because He has been burned to nothing by the fires of human passion, or of the crematoria; and yet the theologically fraught language of the poem suggests that perhaps He nevertheless exists, in some terrific unlooked-for refraction, in man's imponderable capacity to desire, to suffer, to destroy. God is never alluded to in "Noah in the Regions of the Sea." The biblical story has been emptied of divine presence, nothing more remaining than the shadow of the idea of God, for which the supervising bureau-cracy of the contemporary Noah's world is a sad substitute, indeed. Amichai's poem, like Beit-Arié's, includes an explicit declaration that there is no God, but in a very different tone and with very different implications. The beauty of the stars, once a token of God's presence, as in the magnificent creation poem that is Psalm 8, is, in this place where a whole people has been driven out or murdered, camouflage for His abysmal absence.

Nevertheless, at a table far below the deceptive canopy of the night sky, a Christian – "heavy" by metonymic contamination from the piece of ponderous German furniture at which he sits – and a Jew – "light" by way of obvious antithesis to his Christian counterpart, and perhaps because he is not more than a wraith – sit and try to concoct a new religion. This highly elliptical and vaguely absurd scene brings us close to the heart of Amichai's peculiar version of posttraditionalism. The emptiness of the cosmic spaces beyond the stars has been con-firmed by the terrible events whose afterimages flit through the poem. Yet we do not easily dispense with the idea of faith. The imagination pushes, if only in the realm of fantasy, as a gesture of impossible nos-talgia, toward an encounter between Christian and Jew not as mur-derer and victim but as coworkers in the shaping of a new faith after the foundations of faith seem to have been destroyed.

The enigmatic character, the fragmentation of both form and theme, the plain spookiness of Amichai's poem make it an extreme case of the general phenomenon I have tried to describe: as readers, we are left with a sense of uneasiness because uneasiness is one of the important things one has to feel about this subject. The Holocaust has often been reduced to a shorthand of horror—"Auschwitz," boxcars, gas chambers, lampshades, soap. The distinctive value of poetic response is that it subtly resists stereotypes, insists on complexity of feeling and indeterminacy of vision, and unsettles the very frameworks of interpretation that we might otherwise uncritically bring into play. Although the destruction of European Jewry is not an event without precursors, it remains the most unfathomable of experiences in Jewish history. Poetry's special power simultaneously to dislodge and intensify inherited texts, terms, concepts, and values reminds us that all projects for fathoming the event presume to conclude where, for a long time to come, we need to question and to brood.

8/ A PORTRAIT OF YEHUDA AMICHAI (1986)

Yehuda Amichai's home in Jerusalem, looking out over the Valley of Hinnom on the looming crenellated walls and turrets and domes of the Old City, might seem like a perfect vantage point for a Hebrew poet. But Amichai did not choose it for the view. Characteristically, he ended up living there because there was no place else he could afford.

The neighborhood, Yemin Moshe, is now the most exclusive in Jerusalem. Its elegantly renovated stone houses, many of them built in the late nineteenth century, are mainly occupied by artists, galleries, and foreign millionaires. But in the early 1960s, when the city was still divided, Yemin Moshe was perched on the edge of no-man's-land, hemmed in to the east by barbed wire, exposed to occasional potshots from the Jordanian border guards, and, because of these conditions, a half-abandoned, rubble-strewn slum. It was just the sort of neighborhood where a poet, living largely on his schoolteacher's salary and recently separated from his first wife, could meet the rent on a one-bedroom place.

When Amichai moved to Yemin Moshe, he was already regarded in many circles in Israel as the country's leading poet. In the intervening two decades, he has been accorded international recognition unprece-

dented for a modern Hebrew poet. Individual poems have been translated into some twenty languages, and volumes have appeared in German, French, Swedish, Spanish, Catalan, and, most abundantly, in
English with notable frequency since the early 1970s. In May 1986 he
was voted a foreign honorary member of the American Academy and
Institute of Arts and Letters. In the same year, Harper and Row published *The Selected Poetry of Yehuda Amichai*, a generous representation of all his published verse, newly translated by a couple of Americans, Stephen Mitchell and Chana Bloch.

By now, the sixty-two-year-old Amichai, his government pension
and the modest income he still earns from teaching supplemented by
foreign royalties and frequent personal appearances abroad, has com-
fortably settled into his once precarious abode. Work has begun on a
second story of the house, which he now owns. Several years ago, he
had a study built underneath the living room. You get to it by way of a
trapdoor and ladder, at first imagining you are about to descend into a
dank basement. Then, because the house is built into the contours of
a steep hill, you discover a bright and airy book-filled room, with still
another spectacular view, from a point fifteen feet lower, of the Old
City.

There are few places in the world where archeological stratification
is so extravagantly visible. From the window of Amichai's study, you
can see the Ottoman walls of the Old City, the still lofty vestiges of a
Herodian citadel, the two splendid mosques, one of them dating from
the seventh century, a nineteenth-century clock tower that Amichai
insists—convincingly—looks like one of Kaiser Wilhelm's policemen
in his domed helmet, and, down below, the valley where, in biblical
times, the sons of Hinnom offered human sacrifices.

From his earliest poems, archeology has been a primary source of
metaphors for Amichai's perception of the human condition. He sees
both the self and history as an elaborate depositing of layers in which
nothing is ever entirely buried from sight, in which the earliest strata
uncannily obtrude upon the latest. Thus, in his brilliant cycle of poems, "Jerusalem, 1967," the speaker looks out on the Jerusalem landscape:

Above the houses—houses with houses above them. This is all of
history.
This learning in schools without roof
and without walls and without chairs and without teachers
This learning in the absolute outside.
(Translation by Stephen Mitchell)

In an odd way, though Israel is a country obsessed with archeology,
Amichai's use of it as a way of conceptualizing history and self is one
of the things that have set him apart. "I was raised," he told the Israeli
critic Chana Kronfeld in an interview she will include in a forthcom-
ing study of his work, "on two different linear outlooks: the religious
and the Marxist." He has in mind, first, his parents' Orthodox home in
Würzburg, Germany, and the schooling they gave him there. His
Marxist outlook took form after the family moved to Palestine in 1935
when Amichai was eleven, and it was fostered by the Socialist youth
movement, to which most Jewish adolescents belonged in the Palestine of the 1930s and early 1940s. Against such linearity, he suggests,
the notion of archeological stratification has given him a more complex way of conceiving experience in time—and, I would add, a way
that is a sober alternative to the messianic optimism of both traditional Judaism and Marxism.

But archeology has another attraction for Amichai, as he goes on to
intimate in his interview with Chana Kronfeld: "I am drawn to people
who are concerned with real things, like archeologists and geologists.
That is really pure poetry."

The affinity for real things is, in fact, one of the peculiar strengths of
Amichai's poetry and also, I would guess, one of the reasons for its accessibility to so many readers, even when it is formally innovative and
utterly surprising in its leaps of metaphor. His Hebrew is often rich in
soundplay, wordplay, allusion, and other traits of virtuosity that are
not readily evident in translation, and his language is a shifting mixture of colloquial and literary. But the poems are anchored in the con-
creteness of everyday experience through the homey immediacy of
their images: a tricycle left out in the rain, kids' chalk drawings, the
stub of an old theater ticket in a coat pocket, rusty plumbing, a refrig-

erator door. Such objects are used to represent a range of feelings and imaginings all the way from forlornness and love to resurrection and prophetic vision. Meeting Amichai, one quickly senses that, in his daily life, he is a person with an unflagging zest for the tangible particulars of the ordinary world.

Typically, he is up by 6 A.M., while his wife, Chana, his son David, thirteen, and his daughter Emanuella, eight, still sleep. A favorite early morning activity, before he sits down to write until 10 or 11 A.M., is cooking soup or jam, and he is the one who usually buys produce for the family, crossing Jerusalem by bus to the open-air market of Mahaneh Yehuda, armed with plastic net baskets that he will carry back loaded with fruit and vegetables, each variety carefully selected from its own special stall. Keeping a certain distance from the encroachments of technology, he has never learned to drive. He and his wife acquired a little Renault three years ago, and it is she who operates it, cautiously, as a late driver, but competently.

An easy and amiable walker and talker, Amichai loves to explore all the odd and interesting nooks and crannies of the world around him. Within months after the Old City became accessible to Israelis in June 1967, he could take you to the café there that had the best coffee, the little hole-in-the-wall restaurant that served the most ambrosial hoummus, the strangely idyllic Ethiopian monastery, with its cluster of huts, on the roof of the Church of the Holy Sepulcher that was, as he said, "a piece of Africa in the heart of Jerusalem."

Amichai is also an avid soccer fan, although he has favored the more muscle-straining activities of weight lifting, wrestling, and track and field in his imagery. In 1971, when he was spending an academic quarter at Berkeley, I took him to his first American football game, which, because of his infectious enthusiasm for every exotic detail, proved to be the most exciting game I had ever watched. (The home team seemed to share the sense of occasion, pulling a victory out of the fire in the last twenty seconds).

But if Amichai is, in some ways, an irrepressible enthusiast, there is also an element of brooding sadness in the man and his work, sadness about personal loss, aging, mortality, the evanescence of love, and the terrible price exacted by one war after another. He has fought in five, beginning as an eighteen-year-old in the British Army in World War II. When he rose to sudden prominence in Israel with the publication of his first book of verse in 1955, it was partly because he had succeeded better than any of his contemporaries in introducing a new sound into Hebrew poetry, more colloquial, more ironic, more "Anglo-Saxon," as the Israelis say when they mean English-language culture. But his success was also because his articulation of a desperate attempt to cling to the preciousness of private experience, his grasping at love in a landscape of bunkers and barbed wire, spoke so poignantly to the Israeli predicament. In November 1973, a few weeks after the Yom Kippur War, so traumatic for many Israelis, he wrote me: "Again, all of a sudden, my poetry has come back into fashion. Alas for the times when my poetry is in fashion."

The remark is typical in its wry self-deprecation, even at the expense of accuracy. In fact, Amichai's poetry has enjoyed unwaning popularity in Israel since the mid-1950s. Individual volumes of his poems sell between ten thousand and fifteen thousand copies, and the Hebrew collection of his early work, *Poems: 1948–1962*, several times reprinted, has by now sold fifty thousand copies. One should keep in mind that there are considerably fewer than three million readers of Hebrew in Israel, so that the American equivalent of such sales would run to a couple of million copies per book.

Perhaps partly because of his success abroad, which is enough in itself to rouse the suspicions – and jealousy – of any Israeli intellectual, Amichai has had his ups and downs over the years with the local critical and academic establishments. More than one brash young critic has tried to make a reputation by "debunking" Amichai, by demonstrating that his work is nothing but a bundle of tired mannerisms, that his only good poems were written before 1955, and so forth. Though literary fashions change in Israel as elsewhere, these efforts at devaluation have never really taken. There is, admittedly, some unevenness in almost any volume of Amichai's verse, early and late, but for sheer energy of imagination, for the constantly renewed sense of poetry's ability to engage reality, Amichai has no close competitors on the Israeli scene, and perhaps only a few worldwide. Readers of poetry in Israel, relatively far more numerous than their counterparts in America and probably less likely to follow the shifting winds of critical chic, have continued to respond warmly to these qualities in Amichai's work.

Amichai's politics, as far as I can determine, have played no role, positive or negative, in his popularity at home. If Israeli society at large is more or less evenly split between right and left, that symmetry disappears in the community of people likely to read serious literature; there, the decisive majority stands somewhere on the left.

Amichai characterizes himself as a liberal, generally in sympathy with the Israeli Labor movement, and in this he does not differ from most other Hebrew writers. In a society where political issues are so urgent, no writer can avoid some direct involvement in them. From time to time, Amichai has signed petitions or otherwise participated in public gestures of protest on such questions as government policies toward Arabs in the occupied territories and ultra-Orthodox acts of coercion. As a poet, he has shown a willingness to meet Arab counterparts on the shared ground of Arab-Hebrew poetry readings. But, unlike the prominent Israeli novelists Amos Oz and A. B. Yehoshua, he has never been an activist in party politics, has never written political polemics, and remains essentially a private person who confronts politics chiefly in imagining, through some of his poems, how the political realm impinges on private lives. This freedom from ideology may, in fact, be an important reason why his poetry has seemed so meaningful to Israeli readers.

Back in the early 1970s, I witnessed a rather comic dramatization of the bond between Amichai and his Hebrew readers. We had gone together to a big academic conference at the Hebrew University in Jerusalem in order to hear a paper on Israeli avant-garde poetry by a friend of Amichai's. The large classroom in which the session was to take place was filled to capacity. Before the speaker began, the conference facilitator, a young woman who, to judge by her heavy American accent and faltering Hebrew, must have been a recent immigrant, stood up in front of the group, and, surveying the crowded aisles, announced: "These sessions are strictly for those who have registration tags. I am very sorry but whoever has no tag will have to get out of this hall." This is what she meant to say, but instead of *'ulam,* "hall," she said *'olam,* "world."

Her monitorial eye, scanning the front row, lighted on the first tag-less shirt: "You, there," she told Amichai, "get out of this world right now." The poet rose, his face flushed with what must have been the pride of martyrdom. Then the room exploded with imploring cries: "Yehuda, Yehuda, sit down, sit down!" It is characteristic that anyone in Israel with literary interests would be, or would presume to be, on a first-name basis with him. At this point, the chairman of the session, a dour-faced scholar of modern Hebrew literature whom I would have thought incapable of any such theatrical gesture, tore the tag from his own chest and extended it to Amichai.

Later, back at the poet's house, he went over the details of the episode with an unconcealed relish that must have been heightened by a sense of pique over the treatment certain academic critics had given his work. "When she told me to get out of this world," he confessed "that was a great moment for me—all my fantasies that the academic establishment wanted to persecute me were at last publicly realized."

Actually, Amichai has a very friendly relationship with his audience, including many of its academic members. In Israel, he is a celebrity who has never sought that condition and who has managed not to be seduced by it. There are days when his phone seems never to stop ringing: a young poet, asking him to look at a manuscript (he'll probably say yes); a journalist, digging for some piece of literary gossip (he'll politely decline, saving such nuggets for his friends); a kibbutz secretary, inviting him to give a reading (he is almost certain to accept; these are among his favorite audiences); a former student, asking for advice in a personal crisis (he will listen with real sympathy, but what can he do?).

He enjoys some of this because he is a man who likes people, and, in common with most writers, he is gratified by admiring attention. What saves him from any poet-laureate posturing is that, finally, he writes for himself—"to keep myself going," he once said to me—and not for the adulation, and so his place of preference is at his desk, not in the public eye. "I try to stay a civilian," he remarked to me in the same conversation, "to live as a human, not as a poet." Still more pointedly, he commented on his feeling about his work to Chana Kronfeld: "I write about the things that happen to me, not as a poet but as a human being."

Most readers of Amichai are likely to sense in the poetry an appealing quality of unaffected humanity. How that comes about through the artifice of the poem is a complicated question. I suppose almost all poetry begins with a rejection of certain poetic models and an emulation of others, and such choices were clearly important in the creation of a distinctive Amichai voice.

When he began to write at the end of the 1940s, the dominant style in Hebrew verse for more than a generation had been extravagantly literary, sometimes in a histrionic or declamatory fashion, sometimes in a mannered symbolic one. The taste for obtrusive artifice against which Amichai rebelled reflected the peculiar history of modern Hebrew poetry. This body of poetry did not begin with the state of Israel, but almost two centuries earlier, in Germany, during the Enlightenment. There had been, in fact, a continuous tradition of secular Hebrew poetry from 1,000 C.E. onward that flourished in Spain, Portugal, Provence, Italy, and the Netherlands; but this new literary movement, which, during the nineteenth century was to migrate by stages from Central to Eastern Europe and then, with the early phases of Zionism, to Palestine, differed in consciously defining itself as a modernizing, secularist movement.

By the early twentieth century, most signally in the remarkable Jewish literary center in Odessa, in Russia, the new Hebrew poetry reached achievements of the first order of originality. But no one yet spoke the language that the poets used; they themselves culled it from the sacred texts of tradition – the Bible, the Midrash, the Talmud, the liturgy. Even those poets who settled in Palestine and, by the 1920s, adopted Hebrew as their daily language, typically continued to piece together their verse from the purely literary idiom of the sundry traditional texts, recast in the formally symmetrical molds of the Russian poetry most of them had been raised on. For Amichai and his contemporaries, who were the first literary generation since ancient times to use Hebrew as a vernacular, there was a compelling need to break sharply with the immediately antecedent poetic tradition. But the new spoken language alone could not be a sufficient guide: literary models were required that could show how an everyday language might be expressively transmuted into verse.

During his service in the British Army, Amichai discovered by chance a Faber and Faber anthology of modern English and American poetry from Gerard Manley Hopkins to Dylan Thomas. It opened a new horizon of poetic possibilities for him: the influence of both Thomas and W. H. Auden is manifest in his early work, and one still sometimes detects a certain Audenesque wryness in his poems. Rilke is another informing presence for him, occasionally in matters of style — he has written vaguely Rilkesque elegies — but perhaps more as a model for using a language of here and now as an instrument to catch the glimmerings of a metaphysical beyond. (Although Amichai's native language is German, he attended a Jewish school in Würzburg and so was already fluent in Hebrew by the time he immigrated to Palestine.)

Within the Hebrew tradition, Amichai has several times avowed an affinity for two predecessors. Leah Goldberg, a quiet, personal voice among the previous generation of Hebrew poets, who favored musical and balladic forms, meant much to him in his early career. In a poem commemorating her death, he recalls having carried a slender volume of her verse, battered and taped, in the battles of the Negev in 1948–49. Paradoxically, Amichai has also been drawn, from time to time, to the rigorous formal intricacies of medieval Hebrew poetry — he has written some remarkable quatrains, emulating the medieval form — perhaps because they have helped him realize his program of "saying emotional things dryly." A compelling model, not exactly in style but in poetic stance, has been Shmuel Hanagid, the remarkable vizier and commander-in-chief of eleventh-century Granada, whose brooding poems on aging, death, and the terrible arena of politics and war often have a strange modernity, for all their medieval idiom.

Amichai's great gift has been his ability to express the concerns of a somberly mature imagination in a style that could seem — sometimes quite deceptively — simplicity itself. Here, for example, is the opening stanza of "God Has Pity on Kindergarten Children," a poem from his first volume of verse that quickly became, for understandable reasons, one of his most anthologized pieces:

> God has pity on kindergarten children.
> He has less pity on school children.
> And on grownups he has no pity at all,
> he leaves them alone,
> and sometimes they must crawl on all fours
> in the burning sand
> to reach the first-aid station
> covered with blood.
> (Translation by Stephen Mitchell)

The local resonance of these images in an Israel after the costly fighting of 1948–49 hardly needs explaining, but there is also something about the poem, as about many others by Amichai, that makes what is distinctively Israeli in it a deep source of universality. On the surface, these lines are a simple literal statement, proceeding in a geometrically neat series — "saying emotional things dryly" — from the sheltered kindergarten children to the unpitied grownups exposed to the savagery of war. But the poem as a whole requires a double take of figurative rereading as we realize that the initial picture of the bleeding battle casualty crawling for help is also a metaphorical image for all the desperations, public and private, of pitiless adult existence.

Amichai, in fact, often sees a metaphorical equivalence between war and life, each marked by its own terrors, its own necessities for courage and heroic persistence, and it is noteworthy that, on several public occasions, he has characterized poets as "art's combat troops," in contrast to novelists, who enjoy a loftier overview behind the front as "art's generals." The ironic turn of the comparison, it also should be observed, characteristically, turns on Amichai himself, because the poet has written three volumes of fiction. One of them, *Not of This Time, Not of This Place*, published in America in a somewhat abridged

version in 1968, a long, formally innovative novel about the split consciousness of a German-born Israeli after the Holocaust, stands as one
of the remarkable experiments in Hebrew fiction during the last couple of decades.

For Amichai, there is no contradiction between being a combat soldier and writing poetry as a human being rather than as a poet. This is
because we are all engaged in the relentless warfare of living vulnerable lives under the shadow of death, and poetic metaphor is an indispensable weapon in the hand-to-hand struggle with reality. "Metaphor," he told Chana Kronfeld, "is the great human revolution, at least
on a par with the invention of the wheel."

His metaphors are typically drawn, as I have indicated, from the
sort of everyday scenes and objects that were once outside the pale of
poetic decorum. The sorts of connections made through such metaphors are often unexpected, sometimes startling; and, at their best,
they provide either a sharper way of seeing reality or a fresh angle of
vision for coping with it. Thus, in the middle stanza of "God Has Pity
on Kindergarten Children," the speaker, now making the figurative
character of his language perfectly explicit, goes on to wonder
whether God might not at least have some pity on true lovers, giving
them temporary shelter "like a tree over the old man / sleeping on a
public bench." This is, of course, a far cry from the imagery in Psalms
of a sheltering God who is a rock or fortress and the likening of the
lovers to a bum on a park bench suggests rootlessness, vulnerability, a
pathetic lack of dignity. The vaguely Audenesque simile has the force
of a muted prayer, the tentative hope for a transient moment of grace.
It feels authentic because it is free from poetic pretense and theological illusion.

Amichai is a poet who repeatedly takes chances with his metaphors. Ultimately, I don't think this is a matter of poetic principle but
of sensibility. He has a remarkable capacity for childlike playfulness,
even when he is dead serious, and reaching for metaphor is his way of
making sense of a difficult and often daunting world. Sometimes he
overreaches, but I know of few living poets in whose work metaphor
so often seems genuine discovery. At times, the emotional association

between the two spheres metaphorically yoked is clear, though the spheres themselves are not ones customarily thought of together. For instance, he links speech and lunch sandwiches in an early poem about his childhood: "Only my mother's words went with me / like a sandwich wrapped in rustling waxpaper."

Perhaps, more typically, the metaphoric connection produces a shock effect: "God's hand is in the world / like my mother's hand in the guts of the slaughtered chicken / on Sabbath eve"; "Your body is white like sand / that children have never played in"; "Jerusalem stone is the only stone that can / feel pain. It has a network of nerves"; "The air over Jerusalem is saturated with prayers and dreams / like the air over industrial cities. / It's hard to breathe." Occasionally the transformational play of metaphor becomes itself the virtual subject of the poem, as in the wittily erotic tour de force, "The Visit of the Queen of Sheba." Here is a small specimen of exuberant playfulness from the fourth poem of this eight-poem cycle; the lines describe the Queen's voyage northward up the Red Sea to meet Solomon:

> A solitary bird sang
> in the permanent trill of her blood. Rules fell
> from biology textbooks, clouds were torn like contracts,
> at noon she dreamt about
> making love naked in the snow, egg yolks dripping
> down her leg, the thrill of yellow beeswax. All the air
> rushed to be breathed inside her. The sailors cried out
> in the foreign language of fish.
> (Translation by Stephen Mitchell)

This sort of carnivalesque proliferation of metaphor is by no means limited to purely playful pieces. It is prominent, for example, in the long autobiographical poem "Travels of the Last Benjamin of Tudela," which concentrates on more brooding existential themes. But metaphor is only a means, however central, for Amichai to get at the immediacy of experience. On occasion he can renounce it altogether. A vivid case in point is the following brief poem, written in the mid-1970s:

> When I banged my head on the door I screamed,

"My head, my head," and I screamed, "Door, door,"
and I didn't scream "Mama" and I didn't scream "God."
And I didn't prophesy a world at the End of Days
where there will be no more heads and doors.

When you stroked my head, I whispered,
"My head, my head," and I whispered, "Your hand, your hand,"
and I didn't whisper "Mama" or "God."
And I didn't have miraculous visions
of hands stroking heads in the heavens
as they split wide open.

Whatever I scream or say or whisper is only
to console myself: My head, my head.
Door, door. Your hand, your hand.
(Translation by Chana Bloch)

A few years ago, when Amichai gave a poetry reading on the Berkeley campus, this was one of the poems he included. After he finished
reading, he invited, somewhat unusually, questions from the audience. A bearded young man, glaring truculently, asked him if he had
ever fought in any of Israel's wars. "One or two," Amichai answered
quietly. "And did you see God on the battlefield?" the young man
wanted to know. "No, I didn't see God," Amichai responded with a
certain perplexity, "I saw people getting killed."

At this point, the bearded young man delivered himself of a short
diatribe. There was, he conceded, a certain poignant sadness in some
of the poems he had just heard, but he had been told that Amichai was
Israel's leading poet, and if that were true, Jewish historical destiny
had declined to a sorry condition. For where was the perspective of
eternity, the grand vision of Moses and the Prophets, the sense of divine purpose pulsating in the movements of history? Could such a
writer really claim the glorious mantle of Hebrew poetry?

One is accustomed to hearing political speakers attacked from the
audience but not poets, and there was an expectant silence in the
room as Amichai briefly weighed his response. Given the vehemence
of the questioner, one might have anticipated a curt dismissal, or
withering sarcasm. Instead, Amichai answered in the soft, intimately

conversational tone he always uses, even when addressing large audiences. What he said was as good a concise explanation as one could desire of why he writes poetry, how he writes poetry, and why the poetry he has produced is so accessible and seems so often to be serving a needed purpose. These were, more or less, his words to the indignant young man:

What you are insisting on, what you are looking for in poetry, is exactly the sort of phony phraseology with which all the generals and ideologues and politicians pollute our verbal atmosphere. It's precisely against this that a poet has to take a stand, for the job of a poet is to name each thing, each feeling, each experience, plainly and accurately, without pretense. And that's just the point I was trying to illustrate in the poem I read a few minutes ago. When you bang your head, or when it's caressed, what you want to do, as a poet, is to find the right way to say simply, "My head, My head. / Door, door. Your hand, your hand."

AGNON'S PSYCHOLOGICAL REALISM

Psychological realism is one of several different strands in the intricate weave of S. Y. Agnon's work, and at times he seems to have gone out of his way to make it recede into the background. Fabulist, symbolist, satirist, anecdotalist, moralist, adept of the macabre and the supernatural, he often cultivated the public image of pious storyteller, having established his reputation early on with the ventriloquistic traditionalism of tales like "Agunot" (1907) and "The Crooked Shall Be Straight" (1912) in which the archaizing character of his style and narrative stance was most extravagant. Concomitantly, explicit references to European literature in his work are very few and far between, and even then are typically cast in a language that interposes a barrier of seeming incomprehension between the Hebrew writer and foreign notions of literature, as when Agnon identifies Homer as *raban shel paytaney 'umot ha'olam* – the master (or rabbi) of gentile poets (in other contexts the term means Jewish liturgical poets). When questioned about the possible influence of Kafka after receiving the Nobel Prize in 1966, he responded to the interviewer with annoyance, and in a flourish of coy piety, "Influence, influence! Every writer is influenced, but the main thing is what the Holy One Blessed Be He inspires my heart to write."

In his Nobel speech, Agnon confesses to having immersed himself in European writers from the time he learned to read German, but he mentions no names, and again the rhetoric and emphases of the whole text are a continuous gesture of flaunted piety. Only in the posthumously published *Shira* (1971) were readers able to see Agnon deeply engaged with European literature not from a distance of ironic estrangement but as collaborator, rival, and unabashed heir: the novel abounds in weighted references to Goethe, Keller, Nietzsche, Rilke, Stefan George, and is centrally concerned, as the title hints (a woman's name that means "poetry") with the relation between poetry and truth, literature and experience. The issue of influence is especially pertinent to Agnon's psychological realism (*Shira* itself being his crowning achievement in this mode). A scrutiny of his technical procedures and his assumptions as psychological realist make it particularly hard to maintain the notion he often liked to foster that he somehow sprang directly out of the Bible, the Midrash, the commentaries of Rashi, and the tales of the Hasidic masters, without intervention from modern Europe.

Let me propose three writers of the last half of the nineteenth and the early twentieth centuries who I believe played a formative role in Agnon's enterprise as psychological realist. The first of these, Thomas Mann, I will put forth briefly and speculatively while concentrating on the other two. Agnon, as far as I know, is entirely silent on Mann, and Hebrew criticism of Agnon has tended to follow suit. It is unthinkable that Agnon, during his long sojourn in Germany from 1913 to 1924, at a moment when Mann was the dominant figure of German fiction, would have been unacquainted with his work. Mann's experiments in the quasi-musical structuring of narrative through symbolic leitmotiv — as, most famously, in *Death in Venice* (1913) — might well have served as a model for the young Agnon, but, at the very least, they would have reinforced a formal orientation to which the Hebrew writer was in any case disposed. Thematically, the great recurrent preoccupation of the earlier Mann is the alienation of the artist from bourgeois society, the seeming need to sacrifice eros for art, and the intimate relation between art and neurosis, art and disease. This entire cluster of themes is a virtual obsession of Agnon's, from "Agunot" and "Tishrei" (1911) down to *Shira*. Perhaps this affinity between the two writers is no more than a common impulse of the early twentieth-century zeitgeist, though Agnon's thematic exploitation of leprosy in conjunction with the writer's art in *Shira* and in the related story "Forevermore" makes one wonder whether he may not have taken a clue from Mann's use of cholera in *Death in Venice*. And, indeed, as the Israeli scholar Nitza Ben-Dov has recently shown, the gesture at the end of *A Simple Story* (1935) in which the protagonist throws an inordinately large coin to a beggar is an actual quotation of Mann's report of the identical action by Aschenbach in *Death in Venice*.

The other two literary antecedents I want to propose (and this is of course not meant to be an exhaustive list) make their presence felt in his fiction in more clearly demonstrable ways. If Mann was the ascendant figure in the German novel during those crucial years in Germany when Agnon was devoting himself to tireless autodidactic reading in many directions (as his friend Gershom Scholem would later testify), Freud was one of the dominant innovative figures in German-language thought of this period. (Mann himself, we should remember, was abundantly attentive to Freud.) The importance of Freud for Agnon, though hinted at as early as the 1930s by the Hebrew critic Dov Sadan, is just now beginning to be generally grasped. My own awareness of it has been significantly heightened by Nitza Ben-Dov's illuminating work on dreams in Agnon's fiction, and I would also mention useful recent articles by Yael Feldman and Gershon Shaked that deal with psychoanalytic motifs. This particular influence is one that Agnon took pains to hide. The narrator of his short novel *Until Now* (1952) at one point, having reported a dream, professes to be like neither Joseph and Daniel nor their latter-day descendants who claim to know the meaning of dreams. Agnon comes no closer than this in his fiction to explicitly invoking the founder of psychoanalysis, and those of his letters that have been published contain only a couple of brief, facetious references to Freud. An instructive instance of his characteristic procedure of camouflage has been aptly observed by the Agnon scholar Arnold Band. The initial, 1932 version of the story "Another

Face" contains the sentence, "Hartmann was grateful that she did not interpret his dream as would Freud and his circle," which Agnon was careful to delete from the 1941 revision of the story that was subsequently printed in later editions of his collected fiction. Arnold Band identifies the 1930s as the period during which we can assume with confidence that Agnon came to know Freud's work. It was then that he and his wife became good friends with Dr. Max Eitingon, a member of Freud's inner circle; it was then, according to the testimony of their daughter, that Esther Agnon used to read aloud to her husband from Freud's collected works, which were part of her library. But I think there is evidence in the stories themselves of familiarity with Freud even before this period.

From the midpoint of Agnon's extended stay in Germany, Freud begins to emerge as a powerful presence in his fiction: in the ubiquity of dreams and hallucinations, which are characteristically seen as expressions of an individual unconscious, not a collective or archetypal one; in the pervasiveness of neurosis, the repeated perception of thwarted eros as a condition of civilization, the conception of the world as a dark tangle of psycho-sexual determinisms. More specifically, a whole spate of symbols that we now readily identify as "Freudian" are deployed in Agnon's fiction, early and late, and if he may have hit on some of them intuitively, their abundance suggests at least that *The Interpretation of Dreams* offered him certain eminently usable images. Thus, the novella *The Hill of Sand* (1919, based on the earlier "Tishrei"), a story deeply involved with castration anxiety, and, concomitantly, with the poet-protagonist's fear of female sexuality, is a small thesaurus of upward displacements: itinerant Arab tooth-pullers with their ominous pliers are encountered in the Jaffa streets; a playfully aggressive young woman bites off a lock of the hero's hair; later he shocks her by having his hair cropped at the barber's; when he is visited in his room by a certain Miss Eylonit (roughly, Miss Epicene), he nervously lights matches that go out one after another, and she finds a pair of his trousers thrown on his bed, the empty legs dangling.

In a 1962 speech in honor of the critic Dov Sadan, Agnon, after again dismissing any link with Kafka ("he has nothing to do with my soul's root," he observes, invoking a Hasidic concept), mentions seven European writers that touch him deeply: Homer, Cervantes, Balzac, Gogol, Tolstoy, Flaubert, and Hamsun. Of the six novelists in his list, the first three would be associated with various premodernist aspects of Agnon's narrative art (the use of frame-stories and interpolations; the chatty, authoritative narrator; elements of fantasy and the comic-grotesque), while Hamsun has been duly connected by Arnold Band and others with the neo-Romantic vein in Agnon. It is Tolstoy and Flaubert who are most pertinent to his psychological realism, and of the two, there is some evidence that Flaubert loomed especially large. In 1916, just three years before revising "Tishrei" into *The Hill of Sand* and on the verge of the remarkable realist achievements of the 1920s and 1930s, Agnon wrote to his patron, Zalman Schocken, "Flaubert and everything about him touch me deeply. This poet who immolated himself in the tent of poetry [*hayah meimit 'atsmo be'ohalah shel shirah*] . . . deserves that every writer read about him before writing and after writing, and then no book would be desolate" (quoted in Gershon Shaked, *The Narrative Art of S. Y. Agnon* [Hebrew], Tel Aviv, 1973, p. 25).

The testimony of this letter, it should be observed, is a little ambiguous, because the emphasis is not on the novels but on the figure of Flaubert as sacrificial devotee to art and on reading *about* Flaubert. Clearly, at a moment in Hebrew literary history when varying combinations of bombast and effusion were the order of the day, Flaubert's literary ascesis must have appealed to Agnon and, more particularly, the French novelist's ideal of a perfectly wrought, painstakingly refined prose that would usurp the traditional function of poetry (hence Flaubert is referred to as *meshorer*, "poet," an evident equivalent of the German *Dichter*). Agnon may have also been struck by the oscillation in Flaubert between the realist restraint of *Madame Bovary* and *L'Education sentimentale* and the phantasmagoric excess of *Salammbô* and *La Tentation de St. Antoine*, for there is a related pendulum-swing in his own writing. In Flaubert, too, the crisscrossing antagonisms between artist and society, eros and society, that we have already noted, would have been evident to Agnon. The French writer's novels themselves were accessible to Agnon only through German translation, but his fiction from 1919 onward bears abundant signs that he read them attentively. There is at least one explicit borrowing from Flaubert in the 1935 novel, *A Simple Story*, Agnon's most impeccably sustained work of psychological realism. One recalls that in *Madame Bovary*, Emma's departures by coach for her trysts in Rouen with her lover Léon are marked by the presence of a blind beggar who sings an old romantic song of nubile maidens on a summer day. At the end, racked with pain after having taken poison, she hears the voice of the blind beggar singing outside her window, starts up in bed, and expires. *A Simple Story*, also a novel about how the crass materialism of bourgeois society thwarts romantic aspiration, has its own recurrent blind beggar, associated with other motifs of singing in the book. In the course of Hirshl's cure after his psychotic break, the psychiatrist Dr. Langsam tells him about the blind beggars he remembers from his youth who would sing "sweet and lovely songs without beginning or end that made your heart faint away when you heard them" (chap. 19). Hirshl cannot exist in this timeless cycle of ecstasy beyond the burghers' realm where time is money, and he ends by accommodating himself to society. In the penultimate chapter, walking through the snow with his wife, to whom he has become reconciled, he encounters a blind singing beggar and gets rid of him, in that gesture borrowed from Thomas Mann, by tossing him a surprisingly large coin. On the surface, this is a much gentler use of the blind beggar in the denouement than Flaubert's, but the act invokes the most corrosive irony: throughout the novel, coins and those who count or touch them have been hateful; now at the end, Hirshl uses a coin to banish from his life the dream of desire perfectly fulfilled that had driven him to madness.

There are certainly other Flaubertian motifs in Agnon, and perhaps even the use of leprosy in *Shira* and "Forevermore" may have still another source in *St. Julien l'hôpitalier*. What is more pervasive is a matter of technique. The young Agnon in his letters had spoken of the urgency for Hebrew writers to learn how to make readers *see* their subjects instead of using narrators who merely expatiated on them. Since Agnon is only occasionally a visual writer, and since he cites as the Hebrew model for the power of literary seeing the Bible, a corpus which is notable for its avoidance of the visual, what he had in mind is obviously not the descriptive rendering of scene but the narrative closeness, without prominent authorial intervention, to the experiential immediacy of what the characters undergo. For this immediacy, Flaubert had perfected a special narrative technique (in which he was brilliantly followed by Tolstoy among many others)—*le style indirect libre*, or, as I shall call it, using Dorrit Cohn's term, narrated monologue, that is, the conveying through the narrator's third-person perspective of the characters' unvoiced words, their inner speech as they move in the current of experience. By the latter part of the nineteenth century, narrated monologue had become a widely used technique in the European realist novel. In Hebrew, it surfaces in the first decade of the twentieth century intermittently and unevenly in the fiction of M. Y. Berdichevsky and more subtly in the modernist novellas of U. N. Gnessin. It was Agnon, however, among Hebrew writers, who made narrated monologue a prime instrument of consummate artistry, using it not only mimetically, to convey the kinetic immediacy of the characters' experience, but also analytically, to expose through ironic indirection the motives and obscure urges behind their conscious intentions. In this regard, his real breakthrough as a Flaubertian realist in the age of Freud begins in 1919 with the revised version of the novella *The Hill of Sand*.

The oddly named protagonist Hemdat ("desire of," as in the phrase *ḥemdat besarim*, carnal desire) is an aspiring young poet in the new Zionist community in Jaffa, circa 1910. The plot consists of an elaborate erotic hesitation dance between Hemdat and a young woman named Yael Hayot (both her names have animal associations) whom he is tutoring in Hebrew. In the end, nothing comes of their relationship, and she leaves him to his celibacy and his poetry. Here is a characteristic rendering of Hemdat's perception of Yael, from the beginning of the second chapter (the translation is mine):

> His friends suspect him of something of which he is innocent. Hemdat's friends tell him, Yael is a pretty girl and that's why you're drawn to her. Hemdat says to himself, there's nothing whatever to it, it's because of his compassion for her that he tutors her. He's as far from her as east from west. He hasn't yet touched her even with his little finger. It's not that she isn't pretty, or that she doesn't seem pretty to him. On the contrary, her upright carriage and her glowing flesh and her full body and her inner tranquillity always inspire in him a certain feeling of respect toward her. Consider, before he was acquainted with her he used to say she wasn't pretty, and even worse, in her absence he would call her a chunk of meat.
>
> In the evening she came. Limping, she entered his room, dripping wet from the rain.

The hallmark of narrated monologue is the fluidity of narrative perspectives in which it is made to play its crucial role and the frequent ambiguity of borderline between one perspective and the next. The assertion of innocence in the opening sentence here sounds as though it might be a determination of the authoritative narrator, like the report of what the friends say in the next sentence, but as the passage unfolds, we think back to the beginning and realize that the claim of sexual disinterest is narrated monologue, originating in the character, not the narrator. The clearcut shift into Hemdat's train of thought begins with quoted rather than narrated monologue ("Hemdat says to himself . . ."), but after the first few words the language glides into narrated monologue, marked by the use of the third person instead of the first person ("it's because of his compassion for her that he tutors her"). At first thought, the difference between the two narrative stances may seem merely mechanical, but the advantage of the indirect report of monologue is that it becomes tinged, quite misleadingly, with the authority of the third-person narrator (hence the force of the current Hebrew term for this technique, *maba' meshulav*, combined discourse). As such, narrated monologue proves an apt vehicle for the ironic exposure of the gap between the character's perceptions and his motives: it sounds as though it should have the status of objective fact, but a series of small signals – internal contradictions, inadvertencies of word choice, odd or disproportionate emphases – give it away as the character's own strategy of self-deception.

It is easy enough to see how all this works here. From the profession of compassion (rahmanut) and the assertion of antipodal distance, Hemdat is proud to announce to himself that "He hasn't yet touched her even with his little finger," but the inadvertent "yet" intimates what he does not admit to himself, that he would like to touch her, and with more than his little finger. This last clause triggers the reflection on Yael's physical attractions: the movement from upright carriage to glowing flesh and full body tells us where his thoughts are drawn, the final mention of inner tranquillity (literally, "the tranquillity of her soul") being a kind of sop to loftier things. This whole reflex of self-deception culminates in the "certain feeling of respect [kavod]" at the end of the sentence, hardly the emotion suggested by the allure of Yael's body just evoked. In the original, the concatenation of Hemdat's thoughts is marked by a talmudic tonality to which Agnon's archaizing Hebrew readily lends itself, with transitions indicated by terms like 'aderabah, "on the contrary," bo' ure'eh, "consider." The air of deliberative logicality of this language is sharply contradicted by the violence of the thoughts, which swing from the lingering over Yael's appealing body to an earlier, highly defensive perception of her as "a chunk of meat" (the phrase is based on a Yiddish expression that means "worthless young woman," but we might note that Hemdat is a vegetarian). Here, as elsewhere in the novel, there is no explicit narratorial analysis or judgment of the character; instead, Agnon makes us "see" Hemdat by intimating the language the character speaks to himself, which reveals him as a man awash in unconsummated desire that he habitually denies to himself.

I have included in the excerpt the first words of the next paragraph of chapter 2 in order to illustrate how easily Agnon moves from ironies generated by the representation of consciousness to ironies produced by the narrator's formulations. The innocent-looking phrase, "In the evening she came" (ba'erev hi' ba'ah) is taken from Esther 2:14, where it describes the action of each of the beautiful virgins who enters the royal palace to spend a night of amorous trial with the king. Yael's limp is the result of a bad leg that gets a good deal of attention in the story and that, perversely, seems linked with her sexual attractiveness for Hemdat. (Does he see in it, one wonders, among other possibilities, a kind of reassuring counterpart to the impotence he fears in himself?) In the second sentence, although there are no verbal echoes, the rain-soaked lover in the dark at the door may be a situational recollection and reversal of another biblical text – the male lover of Song of Songs who pleads for his beloved to open the door because his locks are wet with the dew of the night. The ironic allusiveness here is indigenously Hebrew, but in a moment we will consider a more elaborate instance in which the seamless integration of vivid, thematically freighted narratorial report with the intimation of the character's consciousness has a truly Flaubertian cast.

First, however, I would like to note that what often distinguishes Agnon's exploitation of narrated monologue from Flaubert's is that the later writer, beyond his interest in evoking the verbal texture of consciousness and, with it, the stratagems by which consciousness thinly veils its own real motives from itself, often uses the technique to lay bare what is buried in the unconscious. We will consider some striking instances of this procedure from *A Simple Story*, but to illustrate how this representation of the repressed is already present in *The Hill of Sand*, let me cite just one brief example. In chapter 3, at a social gathering at Yael's apartment, Hemdat finds himself ill at ease: "Hemdat did not join in the conversation but sat by himself peering at Yael's bed made from oil crates. That bed bore the promise of smashed limbs, not of rest." The use of the deictic "that" ("that bed") is in general one of the few clearcut verbal indicators of narrated monologue since it necessarily signals the character's perspective of location or attitude, not the narrator's. The statement that the fastidious Hemdat makes to himself about smashed limbs is obviously a hyperbole for how uncomfortable the makeshift bed looks to his bourgeois eye. But the violence of smashed limbs is far in excess of the perception of discomfort he is making, and the motor behind that excess is an entirely unconscious associative chain: Yael's bed – sex ("rest" being a cover word) – female sexuality – physical violence – dismemberment – castration. Readers who recall Herbst's erotic nightmares in *Shira* will note that those psychological concerns and something of their method of representation are already present on a miniature scale in *The Hill of Sand*.

In the concluding chapter of the novella, as an introduction to the very last scene, the narrative returns to the thematic space that was its point of departure in chapter 1 – Hemdat's green-shaded room overlooking the Jaffa beach, seemingly removed from the disturbances of carnal existence below.

> His room is on the top floor, and it has five windows. The windows are open all day long and greenish shades the color of the waves of the Nile flap against the windows, and when the shades flap, fringes of light and fringes of shadow form a checkered pattern on the floor. Hemdat paces back and forth the length and breadth of the room. The windows are open in every direction but the door is closed and bolted. Blessed and happy days have come to the world, and Hemdat knows their nature. You won't find him in the streets of Jaffa and you won't meet him on the beach. In the quiet of his home he sits, before his goodly desk. How does Hemdat celebrate the festival of the days? With the offering of his art. Summer has gone now and winds are blowing ever stronger. The eucalyptus trees sway in the garden and shed shriveled leaves. In a corner of Hemdat's room a dry leaf scurries. The wind has borne it.

Unlike our two previous examples, the dominant perspective here is the narrator's, not the character's; but even so, in keeping with the Flaubertian ideal, thematic statement and characterization are conveyed not by explicit commentary but by making us "see" the reported details. The color green is one of the organizing motifs of the novella, working in a way structurally analogous to blue in *Madame Bovary*. Yael's eyes are green; Hemdat's shades are green as "the waves of the Nile" in a kind of mocking mimicry of the world of vegetal life and pulsating desire which they in fact partition off from his bachelor's sanctuary. The top-floor room, open to every side as a post of observation but closed and bolted (the Hebrew phrase, *segurah umesug-eret*, is used in the Bible for besieged Jericho) to all the world, aptly defines Hemdat's relation to life as a withdrawn observer. With the clause "Blessed and happy days have come to the world," which makes more sense as the character's judgment than as the narrator's, and with the first and only indication of inward perception ("Hemdat knows"), we edge into narrated monologue. The shift into the character's perspective is quiet but crucial to the effect of the whole. The language begins to assume the symmetry of a quasi-biblical parallelism that suggests a ceremonial flourish of self-satisfaction on Hemdat's part: "You won't find him in the streets . . . you won't meet him on the beach. In the quiet of his home he sits, before his goodly desk." This suggestion is reinforced by a slight heightening of the diction. The phrase "in the quiet of his home" is in the Hebrew literally "in the tent of his home," and the biblicizing element is drawn out in the next two brief sentences, with the celebration of "the festival of the days" and "the offering of his art [literally, poetry]." The subversion of conscious motive and perception is subtler here than in our previous examples. On the surface, we see a sensitive young man in the loftiness of his verdant retreat expressing a tranquil sense of genuine elation, the poet contemplating the world in the joy of his creation. In point of fact, the story leaves considerable room for doubt as to whether Hemdat has created anything of worth or is likely to do so, and the biblical language here carries a hint of pretentiousness. Hemdat characterizes his poetry as an "offering" or "sacrifice" (*qorban*) to the festival of the days, a metaphor consciously determined by his inclination to see himself as a high priest of art but overdetermined by his unadmitted knowledge of sacrifice in a psychological sense – the sacrifice not of art to life but of erotic life for art.

With the description of scene conveyed by the last four sentences, we move back to the overviewing perspective of the narrator. The beautifully focused nature of these terse concluding notations shows how much Agnon had learned during the decade since the publication of his first, often effusive stories. (The 1911 version of this story contains only a crude sketch of the first two sentences of our passage, followed by a great exclamatory swell of self-consciously emotive meta-phors.) The autumnal winds shaking the eucalyptus trees tell us subliminally that the sun-drenched season of fulfillment has passed for Hemdat without his ever having enjoyed it. The shriveled leaf borne by the winds from without into a corner of the room is at once an emissary of the chill new season and an emblem of Hemdat himself – not the radiant high priest of poetry as he imagines but a poor, barren, desiccated thing cast up by nature into a corner away from the world. The self-characterization of consciousness and the characterization through setting and detail are thus subtly orches-trated to achieve a mastery of realist representation in the manner of the best European practitioners of this mode of fiction.

The novel *A Simple Story*, as I have already intimated, stands in sev-eral respects as the culmination of the techniques of realism Agnon had perfected over the previous fifteen or more years. He would write some short stories in this mode in the forties, but more typically his major fiction from 1939 onward would combine – or occasionally displace – psychological realism with various experiments in symbol-ism and sometimes fantasy as well (*A Guest for a Night, Betrothed, Edo and Enam, Just Yesterday, Until Now*, and, in part, *Shira* as well). The chief psychological material of *A Simple Story* is not neurosis but psychosis, and for this reason evocations of the unconscious exhibit a degree of violence one rarely encounters in *The Hill of Sand*. Dreams now play a more important part, but I would like to concentrate on the representation of waking consciousness, which is carried out, alter-nately, through narrated monologue and the narratorial report of ideas thought and images imagined by the characters. How are we carried from consciousness as it is variously represented to what lies beyond the purview of consciousness? Whether or not Agnon had *The Psycho-pathology of Everyday Life* deliberately in mind, the underlying pro-cess he exploits is free association. The comparisons and metaphors that occur to the characters, the anecdotes of which they are re-minded, and, most vehemently, the intervals of hallucinatory percep-tion to which they are subject, are turned into apertures that open downward to provide glimpses into the dark well of the unconscious.

We shall see how layered and loaded a representation of the psyche this method can produce in the case of Hirshl, the protagonist, but let us begin with a simpler exposure of unconscious motive in Hirshl's father, Boruch Meir. Father and son have come to pay a joint visit to the matchmaker, Yona Toyber, preparatory to the marriage, unsought by Hirshl, that will cause him such grief.

> "What, you too are here?" Yona Toyber asked Hirshl in amazement.
> "So it would seem," replied Hirshl.
> Boruch Meir rubbed his hands with pleasure. Such a comeback had not even occurred to the condemned man in the joke who was asked the same question by the hangman. Boruch Meir was in too good a mood to notice that the comparison was not auspicious. (Translation by Hillel Halkin, New York, 1985, p. 77)

The sentence that begins, "Such a comeback" is of course Boruch Meir's narrated monologue. The narrator's comment about the inauspiciousness of the comparison — the Hebrew is more direct on the issue of figuration, speaking of *mashal* and *nimshal*, figure and referent — makes us think at least twice about the mechanism of association in Boruch Meir's mind. Consciously, he is convinced he has hit on an amusing comparison. Unconsciously, as a father who may know a little about his son and as a man who himself once gave up a love-match in order to marry where his material interest lay, Boruch Meir senses that it is no joke to marry off Hirshl to a woman he doesn't love, that the matchmaker, in complicity with the father, is indeed an executioner. The novelist, moreover, unlike the psychoanalyst, is free to turn a revelatory free association into a datum of the subsequent narrative: the marriage leads to Hirshl's madness, an attempted escape or a kind of suicide from which he must be brought back to the land of the living at the price of an essential part of his selfhood.

Understandably, the free-associative forays into the region of the repressed in Hirshl are more elaborate. Here is a highly explicit, even schematic, instance from early in the novel that nevertheless has real power as a vehicle of thematic definition and psychological character-

ization. The recently engaged Hirshl is at a party of young people, including several of his fiancée's friends.

> Hirshl sat wondering what he was doing there. He felt dazed and de-
> jected. Several times he tried thinking things through and gave up. His
> mind kept jumping until it settled on a story he once was told as a child
> about a man who, finding himself at a wedding, suddenly noticed that
> the bride and groom were made of straw, that the guests were all trolls,
> and that everything in the house was an enchantment. Just as he was
> about to flee for dear life he saw that the wedding ring was real gold and
> decided to take it. No sooner had he done so than the bride stuck out a
> finger and he slipped the golden ring onto it. The trolls roared with laugh-
> ter and so did he. His new wife seized him by his jacket tails and never let
> go of him again. (Pp. 61–62)

The tale remembered from childhood on which Hirshl's distracted
mind settles is of course a pointed allegory of his own situation. The
very explicitness of the correspondences suggests that in this instance
the repressed recognition is almost on the verge of consciousness. But
the recasting of the plot of a marriage imposed for economic reasons
into a fable told to a child gives the realistic story a new dimension of
spookiness; here, as elsewhere in the novel, Agnon the realist strikes
resonances learned on the instrument of his neo-Gothic tales. The
merrymaking friends of the engaged couple, their well-meaning parents, the whole Jewish society of this turn-of-the-century Galician
town, become sinister trolls in a nightmare of illusion, and the bride
and groom lifeless figures stuffed with straw. The fairytale vehicle
makes us feel more acutely what is really at stake in Hirshl's projected
marriage: the moment the man in the story succumbs to the tempta-
tion of gold, he irrevocably loses his soul, even immediately joining in
the mocking laughter of the trolls. (In the dream-logic split, Hirshl is
both the trapped man and the straw-stuffed bridegroom.) The Hebrew
term for the gold ring is *taba'at*, a word formed from the same root as
matbe'a, coin, and thus a particularly apt substitution for the coin
motif that runs through the novel, from the coins Hirshl's parents are
seen counting in their shop near the beginning to the coin cast to the
blind beggar just before the end.

In the middle of the novel, as Hirshl, tormented by his wife's physical presence, edges toward the point of breakdown, the power of the repressed becomes spectacularly evident in the images that occur to him, and there is a perfect psychodynamic continuity between these and his dreams and hallucinations. Thus, tossing about in an agony of insomnia night after night, he is above all fearful that he will awaken his wife, for "The sound of her voice at night was like a nail being driven into a clay wall" (p. 154). This image of Mina as an invasive, penetrating, violating presence reproduces itself in a variety of disturbing ways. If Hirshl escapes her voice at night, he is confronted with it when they get up in the morning and she insists on telling him, between her own yawns, every detail of her dreams.

> Not that her dreams were long; it was more her manner of telling them. If she dreamed of ants, for example, she would insist on describing them ant by ant until his bones shook, as if all the ants she had seen in her dream had stood up on their legs and crawled into his flesh, suffusing him with their odor, which was like that of her bath lotion. He was sure that, when he rolled up his sleeve in the synagogue to bind his tefillin to his arm, everyone would smell it. (P. 124. I have emended the Halkin translation of the second sentence to make it conform more literally to the original, so that the psychological implications of the imagery are more evident.)

The wildness of associative overlaps turned by Hirshl into literal linkages brilliantly conveys the state of mind of a man on the brink of madness. The phantasmal insects of Mina's dream give off the same effluvium as her perfumed body, invade him, impregnate him with an odor he is sure everyone can detect. The psychological power of Hirshl's fantasies is manifested in the freedom with which opposites are fused and polarities reversed. The fragrance of lotion or perfume (*miney sikhah*) becomes the repulsive secretion of ants. Hirshl, a man undergoing a crisis of will and, concomitantly, of virility, has dreamed of murdering "all the cocks in the world" (the Hebrew *gever* means both rooster and man in his sexual aspect). Now, in his similes and fantasies, he repeatedly assumes the passive, penetrable, vulnerable posture of the female while it is the woman who is the driving force.

In all this, I should like to emphasize that one never gets the sense that Agnon, as a consciously Freudian novelist, has merely transcribed from psychoanalytic doctrine a set of "symbols" with clearly identified psycho-sexual equivalencies. On the contrary, the figurative language and the fantasies he invents for Hirshl bear constant witness to a writer boldly following the sinuous turns of ambivalence, the logic of uncanny surprise, of the psychology he is imagining. Fi... offered him, I would say, an orientation toward metaphor, free association, and their relation to the unconscious rather than a definitive lexicon of the unconscious. Let us consider as concluding illustrations two nicely complementary texts that occur in proximity in chapter 25. The first is a daytime dream experienced when the enervated Hirshl briefly dozes off in a doctor's waiting room, and which he mistakes for "thinking"; the second is a chain of insomniac thoughts his mind weaves as he lies in bed waiting in vain for a sedative to take effect.

> What was I thinking? I thought a button had been torn off my jacket and Mina was sewing it back on and I was standing chewing a thread. But was I chewing a thread because it was good for the memory? I'd better spit it out. But the thread refused to be spat out, and instead a sound of snoring came out of my nose. (Pp. 160–61. Here I offer my own deliberately literal translation because the Halkin version smooths out or compresses significant features of the original.)

Behind the mundane realism of a wife setting right a missing button for her husband is an apprehension of emasculation—the button, which is not just gone but is torn off (*nitlash*), is symbolic cousin to the snipped hair and the extracted teeth in *The Hill of Sand*. The chewing of the thread is realistically motivated: by the dictates of superstition, you chew or do something when someone is sewing a button on you in order to ward off the invasion of evil spirits at a moment of magic vulnerability. But the dream-Hirshl is invaded by the thread itself, as the hallucinating Hirshl is invaded by the dreamt ants. Then, as his awareness floats up toward the surface of awakening, he perceives the thread, looping back into his throat and up into the nasal cavity, as the palpable substance of his own snoring. The question about whether chewing thread helps memory is the sort of seeming non sequitur that heightens the psychological conviction of Agnon's writing. According to superstition, chewing the thread prevents the loss of memory while something is being sewn on. But has Hirshl in effect misplaced something important that he is trying to recall in his dream, in his life? If so, it might be Blume Nacht, the woman he has had to give up for Mina, but Agnon, faithful to the elliptical idiolect of the unconscious, is wisely discreet in giving us no more than the baffling, discontinuous question. Another sinuous turn in the passage is the fact that the nightmare experience of the thread that cannot be spat out, which ought to be terrifying (though the dreamer's tone is deliberative and distanced: "I'd better spit it out"), becomes paradoxically the vehicle of longed-for sleep. That paradox is far more conspicuous in Hirshl's night thoughts a couple of pages later.

> What he needed to put him back on his feet was a good cup of coffee. The thought of it made him imagine its smell; the smell of coffee made him picture a hot cup of it, and the beans before and after being roasted, and the sacks of them on the shoulders of the porters who brought them from the station to the store; and the sacks of beans brought to mind the mice that sometimes scampered inside them. Suppose a mouse were inside a sack, and he were to open it, and the mouse were to jump into his mouth, and he were to close it, and the mouse were to remain there half in and half out, with its long tail protruding and tickling the tip of his nose until he fell asleep. (P. 163)

Here we are given a perfectly explicit chain of free associations, the general movement of which will be familiar to anyone who has ever kept himself up at night with restless thoughts. The concatenation from coffee to beans to station to store brings Hirshl to the site of his own imprisonment by the mercantile system, his parents' drygoods store where he has been obliged to accept the destiny of shopkeeper despite himself. The mice in the sacks join company with the novel's crowd of unpleasant or threatening animal images, and the truly hideous notion of the mouse leaping into Hirshl's mouth is the most explicit of the sundry images of quasi-sexual penetration and violation (nails into walls, ants into flesh, thread into mouth) that his mind conjures up. What is astonishing, a token of the surprising leap of authoritative imagination, is that the mouse in the mouth is actually conceived by Hirshl as a moment of bliss, its long tail "tickling," or more accurately, "caressing" his nostrils, and soothing him into the longed-for bourne of sleep. The penetration Hirshl so often seems to fear is also, at some substratum of the psyche, a consummation devoutly wished. If he could only give up his tortured, frustrated maleness, if he could only yield to the pure passivity of surrender (surely a male fantasy about the female role!), he would at last be at peace. The model for this fantasy is sexual, but, in terms of the large social themes of the novel, its ramifications extend far beyond what the protagonist would like to do or have done to him in bed: the inherent conflict between individual fulfillment and the inexorable demands of clan, class, and cash-nexus raises fundamental issues of will, assertiveness, the precarious struggle for personal values, all of which founder in the romantic, familial, and social dilemmas of the protagonist.

There is one formal feature of all the illustrative texts we have reviewed that is worth noting, for it is a hallmark of Agnon's project as psychological realist. His subject is typically souls in anguish, torn by violent inner stresses that in another literary sensibility would logically lead to stylistic wailing and moaning and gnashing of teeth. But from Flaubert — and perhaps in another way, from midrashic narrative as well — he learned the lesson of restraint, the power of understatement. The dreaming Hirshl conveys the details of his nightmare as though he were scrutinizing a problem of biblical exegesis. The narrator reports to us Hirshl's free associations, link by link, without adjectival heightening or adverbial flourish, as though they were pure factual inventory. The climactic surprise of the horrific turned soothing in the coffee-mouse passage is prepared for in the odd suppression of affect in what precedes it.

Throughout Agnon's work, such cultivated dissonance between manner and matter is still more apparent in the Hebrew, with its rabbinic resonances and its classicizing poise a millennium-and-a-half removed from the historical location of the characters. Only the Hebrew language could make so pervasive a presence of the archaic possible in modern realist prose. And yet, what finally unites Agnon with a tradition of European realism from Flaubert and Tolstoy onward is the underlying sense of a world threatening terrifically to come apart at the seams but held together in the firm clasp of art, where the most subtle techniques for the dramatization of consciousness and the intimation of what lies at its borders and below it become a highly wrought, orderly vehicle for the conveyance of psychic undoing and disorder.

S hira is S. Y. Agnon's culminating effort to articulate through the comprehensive form of the novel his vision of the role of art in human reality. It engaged him – with long interruptions, during which he devoted himself to shorter fiction – for almost a quarter of a century. On his deathbed, in 1970, he gave his daughter instructions to publish the novel with Book 4 still incomplete. Posthumously, the text of *Shira* remains unstable. The first Hebrew edition in 1971 ends with the fragmentary ninth chapter of Book 4, which includes Herbst's musings on the professor of medicine who injects himself with a dangerous disease in order to find a cure (a historical figure at the Hebrew University, Shaul Adler), and breaks off with the narrator's declaration that Shira has disappeared and cannot be found. A subsequent edition in 1974 appended the brief episode Agnon had marked in manuscript as "Last Chapter," in which Herbst joins Shira in the leper hospital; this ending was originally intended to conclude Book 3 but was set aside when Agnon went on to write a fourth book. In 1978, another substantial episode, like "Last Chapter" incorporated in the English version, was published: corresponding in fictional time to chapters 8–19 of Book 3, it prepares the way for Herbst's discovery of Shira in the leper hospital and also explores a narrative possibility not raised elsewhere – Herbst's confession of his infidelity to his wife.

Incomplete as it is, and even with some signs of uncertainty in its digressive and repetitive patterns, *Shira* is a remarkable work. The psychosexual realism – most strikingly evident in Herbst's guilt-ridden, violence-prone, sado-masochistic dreams and fantasies – surpasses anything else Agnon did in this vein. What may have prevented him from finishing the book was that beyond any aim of realistic representation of psyche and social milieu, Agnon wanted to imagine in concrete novelistic detail the ultimate relation of art (or "poetry," the meaning of Shira's name) to truth, or, in regard to genre, to pass through the dense medium of realism to allegory, and that was a consummation that eluded him.

It may be helpful to place *Shira* in Agnon's chronological development as a novelist. His earliest Hebrew fiction (there had been a few Yiddish stories before) was published in the half-dozen years after his arrival in Palestine from Galicia in 1907 at the age of nineteen, and consisted entirely of short stories and novellas. Many of these were in the subtly ventriloquistic mode of a traditional Hebrew teller of tales, and it was this identity that figured in most readers' minds as Agnon rapidly made himself a commanding figure in Hebrew prose. Characteristically, his artfully archaizing novella set in premodern Galicia, *And the Crooked Shall Be Straight* (1912), was widely perceived in these years as his emblematic achievement. In 1913 Agnon left Palestine for Germany, ostensibly for a brief stay, but the war and a variety of personal reasons held him there till 1924. It was during the first few years of his German sojourn that he arrived at artistic maturity, rigorously revising his often effusive early stories in a precise, understated, classicizing prose that would remain his hallmark. Shortly after the war, he was working on his first novel, an autobiographical fiction he called *In the Bond of Life*. Though he announced in a letter written in 1920 that it would soon be in print, he must have had difficulties with it because it was still in manuscript in 1924 when it was destroyed in a fire that devastated his apartment in Homburg, and Agnon never attempted to reconstruct the book. His first long integrated work, *The Bridal Canopy* (1931; English trans., 1967), is only marginally a novel, because it reverts to the medieval and Renaissance form of the framestory – the peregrinations of a protagonist and his companion – into which is introduced a variegated abundance of anecdotes, fables, tall tales, and the like.

Meanwhile, Agnon continued to write realistic short fiction far removed from both the eighteenth-century setting and the formal traditionalism of *The Bridal Canopy*, and this involvement in social and psychological realism culminated in his first proper novel, *A Simple Story* (1935; English trans., 1985), a book more restricted in scope than the novels that would follow but, in the rendering of the evolution of a psychosis and its ironically qualified cure, probably the most flawlessly sustained of all his novels. From this point on, though he continued to experiment with different modes of short fiction, from anecdotal and reminiscent to surrealist and symbolic, his commitment to the capaciousness of the novel form was clear. In 1939, writing with uncharacteristic rapidity, he produced *A Guest for the Night* (English trans., 1968), his personal confrontation, on the eve of the Second World War, with the inward dying of European Judaism that he had witnessed after the First World War. In 1945 he brought out an even more ambitiously original novel, *Just Yesterday* (still untranslated), set in the Palestine he had encountered as a very young man, in which he combines historical realism with intricate symbolism and tragic-grotesque humor (some of the most remarkable chapters, initially composed in the early thirties, follow the canine viewpoint of a Jerusalem mongrel named Balak, who proves to be the most philosophically reflective and the most engaging character in the book).

In each of the three novels Agnon published from 1935 to 1945, he had found ways to go strikingly beyond his previous work in fashioning new fictional forms and in sounding a wide range of themes. It was clearly his intention to go beyond himself once again in *Shira*, and he apparently set to work on the new novel not long after the appearance of *Just Yesterday*. Between 1949 and 1952, he published chapters of *Shira* in a literary yearbook issued by the newspaper *Ha'aretz*, material corresponding to most of Book 1 and Book 2 of the novel as we have it. The excitement roused in Hebrew literary circles was then frustrated as Agnon confined the continuation of *Shira* to the privacy of his drawer, pursuing other projects in print. In 1966, after he received the Nobel Prize, he allowed two more chapters to appear, and, with failing physical powers, he was working on *Shira* in his last years, still hoping to forge it into what it would in any case, even incomplete, prove to be – his great last testament as a writer.

Shira is at once Agnon's fullest invocation of the nineteenth-century European novel and a deliberate modernist demonstration of the collapse of the thematic concerns and formal strategies of the nineteenth-century novel. Adultery as an attempted escape from the flatness and the stifling routine of bourgeois society is, of course, one of the two or three great recurrent themes of the traditional novel. One could not have chosen a more thoroughly bourgeois realm in the Palestine of the 1930s than the milieu of the Hebrew University with its predominantly German-Jewish professorate, where propriety, conformism, industriousness, self-importance, and social status were the governing values. Agnon, who lived on the margins of the Hebrew University, some of his best friends being members of its faculty, knew this world well and rendered it in his last novel with a shrewd satiric eye. *Shira*, however, turns out to be something quite different from a latter-day Hebrew reprise of *Madame Bovary* and *Anna Karenina* in an academic setting. Herbst, unlike Flaubert's Emma, does not "discover in adultery all the platitudes of married life" but, on the contrary, finds that a fleeting carnal encounter with an unlikely object of desire opens up vertiginous new perspectives, makes bourgeois hearth and home unlivable for him, impels him in ways he is hardly conscious of to do something radically other with his life.

The background of political violence is one of the keys to the difference between *Shira* and the tradition of the European novel that it recalls. The bourgeois academic world from which Manfred Herbst derives is not a fixed datum of social reality, as would be the case in a nineteenth-century novel, but is seen instead as a fragile choreography of complacent social rituals on the brink of a historical abyss. The novel is set in the late thirties, in the midst of the murderous Arab attacks on the Jewish population of Palestine that began in 1936. The ideological tension between Jewish militants, like the underground group to which Herbst's daughter Tamara belongs, and the pacifists of the Brit Shalom organization at the Hebrew University, is frequently invoked. On the European horizon that has the most urgent thematic relevance to all that transpires in the Jerusalem setting of the novel, Herbst's German homeland is preparing the machinery for genocide. In a world moving rapidly from episodic terror to systematic mass murder on the most unprecedented scale, mere private experience – the staple of the classic novel – dwindles to insignificance. Adultery can no longer be even the illusory personal adventure it was in nineteenth-century fiction, and the very premise of the linear plot of the novel of adultery is called into question: Herbst's involvement with Shira cannot go anywhere as a developing chain of fictional events; instead, he circles around and around the idea of Shira, or, what amounts to the same thing, around what Shira's disturbing presence has released within him.

Let me state this in terms of the quest for knowledge that is a central issue in the novel. Herbst and his fellow cultivators of the grove of academe, equipped with their index cards and bibliographies and learned journals, sedulously pursue the most esoteric and distant objects of knowledge – the burial customs of ancient Byzantium, the alphabets of long-lost languages. The purported sphere of these objects of knowledge is history, but do these historical investigations, beyond their utility in advancing the careers of the investigators, tell us anything essential about the historical forces that are about to move the German nation to gun down, gas, and incinerate millions of men, women, and children? The European perpetrators of these horrors are, after all, at least in part products of the same academic culture as that of Herbst and his colleagues. The most troubling question a Jewish writer after 1945 could raise is variously intimated here, particularly in Herbst's nightmares and hallucinations: Could there be a subterranean connection between forces at work, however repressed, within the civilized Jew and the planners and executors of mass murder who are, after all, men like you and me? At the beginning of the novel, Herbst is unable to write that big second book which will earn him his professorship because he has a writer's block. As the effects of his exposure to Shira sink in, he is unable to write it because it has become pointless, such knowledge as could be realized through it felt to be irrelevant. Instead, Herbst hits on the desperate idea of writing a tragedy, for his experience with the radical ambiguity of eros in his involvement with Shira/Poetry leads him to sense that art, unlike historical inquiry, has the capacity to produce probing, painful self-knowledge, and is able to envisage history not as a sequence of documented events but as a terrible interplay of energies of love and death, health and ghastly sickness. Herbst, with his habits of academic timidity, his hesitant and unfocused character, may not ever be capable of creating such exacting art, but he is ineluctably drawn to the idea of it.

The underlying concern with the nature of art in *Shira* is reflected in its wealth of references – elsewhere in Agnon's fiction, scrupulously avoided – to European writers: Goethe, Nietzsche, Balzac, Rilke, Gottfried Keller, Stefan George, not to speak of the Greek tragedians and their German scholarly expositors whom Herbst reviews in his quixotic attempt to write a tragedy (ostensibly, a historical drama set in the Byzantine period but unconsciously a reflection of his own agonizing erotic dilemma with Shira). From one point of view, this is a novel about the impossibility of tragedy in the modern age, and especially after the advent of Hitler – that is to say, the impossibility of a literary form that assigns meaning to suffering, or represents an experience of transcendence through suffering. In consonance with this concern with tragedy, a good deal of weight is given to Nietzsche's notion in *The Birth of Tragedy* of the roots of the genre in an experience of violent primal forces contained by artistic form – Herbst, preeminently a "Socratic" man in Nietzsche's negative characterization of German academic culture, at one point runs across a first edition of *The Birth of Tragedy* in an antiquarian bookshop.

Another manifestation of Agnon's preoccupation here with the way art illuminates reality is the attention devoted to painting – again, a thoroughly uncharacteristic emphasis in his fiction. Three painters figure significantly in the novel: Rembrandt and Böcklin, who recur as motifs in connection with Shira, and the anonymous artist from the school of Breughel responsible for the stupendous canvas of the leper and the townscape (III:16) that constitutes Herbst's great moment of terrifying and alluring revelation. A look at how the three painters interact in the novel may suggest something of what Agnon was trying to say about art, and perhaps also why his way to a conclusion of the novel was ultimately blocked.

If art, or poetry, is a route to knowledge radically different from the academic enterprise that has been Herbst's world, Agnon sees as its defining characteristic a capacity to fuse antinomies, to break down the logically marked categories—Herbst's boxes full of carefully inscribed research notes—presupposed by scholarly investigation. The Breughelian painting Herbst discovers at the antiquarian's is a multiple transgression of the borderlines of reason, and that, he realizes, is the power of its truthful vision. The leper's eye sockets are mostly eaten away by the disease, yet they are alive and seek life—a paradox that re-enacts the underlying achievement of the painter, "who imbued the inanimate with the breath of life." The medium of the painting is of course silent, but Herbst, contemplating the warning bell held by the leper, experiences a kind of synesthetic hallucination, hears the terrible clanging sound, and feels the waves of the disease radiating out from the leper's hand. The painting from the school of Breughel, as I have proposed elsewhere,* is in its formal and thematic deployment a model for the kind of art embodied in *Shira* itself: in the foreground, the horrific and compelling figure of the diseased person, intimating an impending cataclysm; in the background, half out of focus, the oblivious burghers complacently going about their daily pursuits. Agnon gives us not only the artwork but also an exemplary audience for it in Herbst. The historian of Byzantium is mesmerized by the painting in a paradoxically double way: "he looked at it again and again with panic in his eyes and desire in his heart." The painting at once scares him and translates him to an unwonted plane of experience because it both speaks eloquently to a universal truth of human experience and gives him back a potent image, of which he is scarcely conscious, of his own life.

Seeking relief from the terrible intensity of the Breughelian painting, Herbst flips through a stack of Rembrandt reproductions and comes to

---

*"A Novel of the Post-Tragic World," in my book, *Defenses of the Imagination* (Philadelphia, 1977).

The Night Watch, on which he dwells. Rembrandt would seem to present a kind of art antithetical to that of the anonymous painter from the school of Breughel. The narrator tells us that Herbst now experiences a sense of melancholy accompanied by "inner tranquillity" (*menuḥat hanefesh*, literally, "soul's rest"), a tranquillity usually identified as harmony but which he, the narrator, prefers to associate with the illumination of knowledge. The opposition, however, between Rembrandtian and Breughelian art rapidly dissolves, like most of the key oppositions in the novel. To begin with, *The Night Watch* immediately makes Herbst think of Shira, who had been looking for a reproduction of the painting, and she is doubly associated with disease – the wasting disease which by this point we suspect she has contracted, and her hapless lover's disease of the spirit manifested in his obsessive relationship with her. But a few minutes later in narrated time, Herbst suddenly realizes that his memory has played a trick on him, or, in the psychoanalytic terms never far from Agnon's way of conceiving things from the thirties onward, he has temporarily repressed something. It was not *The Night Watch*, with its beautifully composed sense of confident procession, that Shira wanted, but another Rembrandt painting, *The Anatomy Lesson*. The clinical subject of the latter painting might of course have a certain professional appeal to Shira as a nurse, but what is more important is that its central subject is not living men marching but a cadaver, and thus it is linked with the representation of the living-dead leper in the anonymous canvas.

Death as a subject, in turn, connects Rembrandt with Böcklin, the artist responsible for the painting of the death's-head that Shira keeps in her apartment. Arnold Böcklin, a Swiss painter much in fashion in Central Europe toward the end of the nineteenth century (Stefan George wrote a poem about him), provides one of the teasing keys to *Shira*. Böcklin had a pronounced preference for mythological and allegorical topics, often rendered with a sharp realism of detail, and in pursuing this interest he repeatedly devoted emphatic attention to those figures of classical mythology associated with a riot of sensuality – Pan, satyrs, centaurs, Triton disporting himself with a Nereid. He also produced two versions of an allegorical painting that is particularly pertinent to the central thematic complex of *Shira*: entitled *Poetry and Painting*, it shows two female figures on either side of a fountain (presumably, the Pierian spring), Poetry on the left, naked to the waist, leaning on the fountain's edge; Painting on the right, enveloped in drapery, dipping one hand into the water while with the other she holds a palette. Interestingly, Böcklin never did a painting of a skull, if one can trust the testimony of the comprehensive illustrated catalogue of his paintings published in Berne in 1977.* He was, however, much preoccupied with death, which he characteristically represented in a histrionic mode that has a strong affinity with Symbolist painting. One scene he painted a few times was *The Island of Death*, in which the island looms as a spooky vertical mass against a dark background, with a small boat approaching it in the foreground, rowed by a presumably male figure, his back to us, while a female figure in white stands erect in the boat. One of his last paintings, *The Plague* (1898), exhibits a more brutally direct relevance to *Shira*: a hideous female figure, with large wings and grotesque tail, yet more woman than monster, swoops down over the streets of a town.

The reproduction that hangs on Shira's wall might possibly be one of *Self-Portrait with Death as Fiddler* (1872). It is conceivable that Agnon simply forgot the self-portrait and concentrated on the skull when he introduced the painting into his novel, but given his frequently calculating coyness as a writer, it seems more likely that he deliberately suppressed the entire foreground of the canvas. In the foreground, Böcklin, wearing an elegant dark smock, stands with palette in one hand and brush in the other, his trim beard delicately modeled by a source of light from the upper left, his lively lucid eyes intent on the canvas he is painting. Behind him, in the upper right quadrant of the painting, virtually leaning on the painter's back, death as a leering skull with bony hand—rendered in the same precise detail as the fig-

* The Israeli critic Nitza Ben-Dov, however, has discovered a Böcklin death's head not included in the Berne catalogue. Either Agnon knew this painting or invented something like it from bits and pieces of other paintings by Böcklin.

ure of the artist—scrapes away on his fiddle. That missing artist absorbed in his work who stands in front of the figure of death is, in one respect, what *Shira* is all about.

Death is, I think, a specter of many faces in this somber, troubling novel. It has, to begin with, certain specific historical resonances for the period of the late 1930s in which the action is set. In the two decades since 1914, death had given ample evidence of having been instated as the regnant zeitgeist of the century. Herbst recalls wading up to his knees in blood as a soldier in the great senseless slaughter that was the First World War. The novel begins with mention of a young man murdered by Arabs, and in these days of organized terrorist assaults and random violence against the Jews of Palestine that began in 1936, there is a repeated drumbeat of killings in the background of the main action. On the European horizon, German Jews are desperately trying to escape, many of them sensing that Germany is about to turn into a vast death trap. But beyond Agnon's ultimately political concern with the historical moment as a time of endemic murder, he is also gripped by the timeless allegory of Böcklin's painting: every artist, in every age, as an ineluctable given of his mortal condition, works with death fiddling at his back, and cannot create any art meaningfully anchored in the human condition unless he makes the potency of death part of it, at once breathing life into the inanimate and incorporating death in his living creation. Agnon was nearing sixty when he began work on the novel and an octogenarian when he made his last concerted effort to finish it, and it is easy enough to imagine that he saw himself in Böcklin's attitude as self-portraitist, the grim fiddler just behind him.

Herbst takes due notice of the Böcklin painting in Shira's apartment, and he is several times bothered by an oddly literal question about it: "Did Böcklin paint it from a model or from his imagination? Why do I ask? Herbst wondered about himself" (I:29). Why, indeed, should so sophisticated an intellectual trouble himself about whether the painter used a model or not? The question, it should be observed, makes somewhat better sense if one keeps in mind not just the skull but both figures in *Self-Portrait with Death as Fiddler*, for then, since Böcklin demonstrably used himself as the model for the painter, one might begin to speculate about the "source" for the macabre fiddler standing behind the painter, the very hybrid nature of the composition putting to the test any simple mimetic conception of art. A couple of paragraphs later in the same chapter, a clue, or at least a dangling possibility of connection, is provided for Herbst's question. Again he asks himself whether Böcklin worked from a model or from his imagination, but this time he decides firmly on the latter alternative when he recalls that Böcklin "complained that he never had the chance to draw a woman from life because his wife, who was Italian, was jealous and wouldn't allow him to have a model in his studio." There is an instructive overlap, then, between painting eros and painting thanatos from the imagination rather than from a model. The particular link is important enough for Herbst to pick it up again explicitly in a dream somewhat later in the novel (II:7). In the dream he accompanies his daughter Tamara to Greece, where she means to undertake a study of verse meters (the word *shira* is used here for poetry). The father is glad to have gone with his daughter on the trip, "for otherwise she would have seen him walking with Shira, which was not advisable, because Henrietta was in collusion with the wife of a teacher from Beit Hakerem. They agreed to prohibit their husbands from bringing other women to their studios, declaring, 'If they want to draw — let them draw skulls.' " One notes that Böcklin's allegorical pair, *Dichtung und Malerei*, Poetry and Painting, follow in quick sequence in the dream.

Agnon gives one further twist to the Böcklin painting by turning it at one point into a kind of reversed portrait of Dorian Gray: as Shira visibly deteriorates, the painting deteriorates with her and so its artificial deathliness becomes progressively more lifelike: "The picture became so darkened that it would frighten you, as though a real skull were staring at you" (II:2). Agnon never entirely renounced the macabre interests of his early neo-Gothicism, and though here the ghastly correspondence between painter and owner is given a perfectly plausible explanation — as Shira neglects herself, she neglects her possessions and no longer bothers to dust the painting — troubling thoughts are stirred about the status in reality of the artwork. Its origins, or at least the origins of the part of the Böcklin painting mentioned in the novel, are not in the representation of a model but in the artist's imagination, and yet the unforeseen intercourse between painting and experience produces a spectral affinity between the two, imbuing the artwork with an air of reality the artist himself had not given it.

Let us try to pull these strands together and consider the kind of conclusion to which Agnon wanted them to lead. Shira, hard-bitten, mannish, unseductive, coldly imperious, neither young nor pretty, seems an unlikely candidate either for the focus of an erotic obsession or for the symbolic representation of Poetry. It strikes me, however, that all these unappetizing traits are precisely what makes her the perfect conduit to carry Herbst from the realm of scholarship to the realm of poetry. Agnon's figure for Poetry is no classical maiden in decorous dishabille. Art as he conceives it is a violation of all the conventional expectations of bourgeois rationality. In Freudian terms, the roots of art are in the premoral realm of polymorphous perversity. It is hard to reconcile anything in the character of Shira with ordinary notions of the good and the beautiful, and once Herbst has learned something about her bizarre sexual history, the initial ambiguity of identity between female and male that he perceives in her is compounded by others in his fantasies: Shira is both the rapist and the raped, the wielder of terrible weapons and the dismembered female victim, the nurturer of mothers and infants and the asocial disrupter of families, nurse and source of contagion. Sexually, she clearly appeals to Herbst because she is everything that his faded blonde, maternal, sweetly solicitous wife is not, and in the thematic logic of the novel, it is necessary that he be detached from the complacencies of the haven of domesticity in order to be inducted into the soul-trying realm of poetry. The novel stresses the indissoluble bond between poetry and eros, because in Agnon's view what art does is to give the revelatory coherence of form to erotic energies (the affinity with both Nietzsche and Freud is not accidental), and, conversely, the many-faced spirit of eros, both god and monster, is the very motor-force of art. It is instructive that Agnon's major fiction before *Shira* repeatedly focuses on some form of gravely impaired male sexuality (*A Simple Story, Just Yesterday;* novellas like *The Hill of Sand* and *Betrothed*); only in this novel is there emotionally affecting consummation—"Flesh like your flesh will never be forgotten"—however elusive the object of desire subsequently proves to be.

But the most crucial crossing of opposites associated with Shira is the wedding of health and sickness, love and death. At the beginning, the freckle-like protuberances on Shira's cheeks seem to be merely a token of her mannish unattractiveness; eventually, we realize that they were an early sign of her leprosy, and so the death's-head on her wall becomes an emblem of the fate to which she is consigned, in which Herbst will finally join her. It is reasonable to assume that Agnon, who made a careful study of Freud in the 1930s and probably read him episodically earlier during his sojourn in Germany, followed Freud in positing eros and thanatos as the two universal driving forces of the psyche. A couple of the passages we have glanced at establish an eerie equivalence between the two. If Böcklin, Herbst reasons, was obliged to use only the power of his imagination for the female figures he painted, the same must be true for his painting of the skull. And if Herbst in his dream, constrained like Böcklin by his wife's jealousy, is denied access to female models, he is invited to substitute bony death for woman's flesh as the subject of his art. In the end, no model is required for either because love and death are so deeply seated in every one of us, constituting the matrix of all our human imaginings.

A small point in Agnon's Hebrew makes the force of his ramified use of painting particularly clear. The standard Hebrew verb "to paint," *tzayer*, is also the verb Agnon uses for "to imagine." A chief reason for Herbst's failure to write his tragedy is that he is too fastidious to imagine, or literally "paint to himself," the concrete suffering of the leper who figures centrally in its plot. "Herbst was afraid to immerse himself in that sickness and explore it, to picture various aspects of leprosy, such as how lepers behave toward each other or how they function in conjugal terms" (II:17). The true artist is the person, like Rembrandt of *The Anatomy Lesson*, like the anonymous painter of the school of Breughel, and like Böcklin, who looks on death and disease clear-eyed and unflinching, just as we see the face of Böcklin in his self-portrait serenely scrutinizing his canvas.

If the artist's credo put forth by *Shira* is in one respect distinctly modernist, embracing the idea of art as an unflinching "technique of trouble," in R. P. Blackmur's phrase, it also has an oddly medieval feeling. Herbst is a historian of Byzantium versed in the ascetic practices of the early Christians, and the novel draws explicit parallels between the monastic renunciation of worldly life and the withdrawal to the leper hospital that Herbst will chose as his final fulfillment. In some of his earlier fiction, Agnon had set up a simple alternative between art and eros, depicting protagonists who renounce the gratification of desire in the name of the pursuit of art. Here, on the other hand, desire joins hands with art in the magic circle of imminent death, removed from the shallow egotism and the complacent self-deceptions of everyday social existence. This is chiefly what I had in mind earlier when I proposed that in *Shira* Agnon seeks to move through realism to allegory. And this, I suspect, was precisely the problem that bedeviled him for nearly two decades after the initial élan that produced Books 1 and 2. How was he to take Herbst, a figure with a certain academic pedigree, a family history, individual work habits and domestic tics, and translate him into the symbolic sphere where poetry, desire, and death were one; and what face could Shira, hitherto also a novelistic character with an individual sensibility and a personal history, show in that ultimate locus of thematic convergences, withdrawn from the worldly realm? There is a structural analogy, though I am not proposing any influence, between the ending of *Shira* and the ending of Stendhal's *Charterhouse of Parma*. Stendhal, too, sought to transport a hero trammeled in the petty machinations of worldly life to a privileged sphere of lofty withdrawal from the world, and though his novel never actually breaks off like Agnon's, most critics have felt that the conclusion of this masterpiece of European fiction is huddled, leaping too suddenly from all the complications of the court of Parma to the contemplativeness of the monastery at the very end. Herbst's planned route to the monastic leprosarium is persuasively traced by Adiel Amzeh, the scholarly protagonist of the remarkable story "Forevermore," which Agnon originally wrote to include in *Shira* and then decided to publish separately. In the fuller dimensions of the novel, he was unable to find a solid fictional bridge on which Manfred Herbst could cross over from his home and wife and children and academic tasks to that ghastly consecrated realm where a disease-ridden woman whose name means Poetry could offer him more than the world ever could. The result was a plot in which after a certain point the central character can only turn and turn again in the circuits of his one obsession, circling back on the apartment where Shira is no longer to be found, revolving in his mind the idea of the tragedy he would write and the memory of the flesh that cannot be forgotten, which are but obverse sides of the same lost coin.

There are certain works of literature that are finally stymied by the bold effort of the writer to pursue a personal vision beyond the limits of precedent and genre. Stendhal's *Charterhouse* is a memorable case in point; another, still closer to *Shira* in its actual incompletion, is Kafka's *The Castle*. Confronted with this order of originality, most readers, I think, will be content with the splendid torso, however much they may regret the absence of the fully sculpted figure. In *Shira* the hero's final way to the place of poetry and truth, where death hones desire, is indicated rather than fictionally imagined. But Herbst's descent into an underworld of eros and art, enacted against the background of Jerusalem life in the gathering shadows of a historical cataclysm of inconceivable proportions, is so brilliantly rendered that *Shira*, even without an ending, even with its flaws of meandering and repetition, deserves a place among the major modern novels.

11/ KAFKA'S FATHER, AGNON'S MOTHER, BELLOW'S COUSINS

C ritics of Hebrew literature have long been tantalized by the question of whether it should be seen chiefly in its own cultural context or whether it needs to be set in what might be called a perspective of Jewish comparative literature. A generation ago, the influential Israeli critic Dov Sadan emphatically argued for the latter alternative, proposing that Hebrew literature, at least in its European phase, was an inextricable element of a trilingual literary configuration – Hebrew, Yiddish, and the literature written by Jews in the language of their particular European milieu. This is obviously one of those questions that can never be really resolved because the answer you come up with depends on which aspects of the literature you have in mind. If you are concentrating on issues of style, imagery, allusion, the use of mythic *topoi*, then the "vertical" links between modern Hebrew literature and its medieval and biblical antecedents will often be more decisive than its connections with contiguous Jewish literatures in other languages. If you are thinking (as Dov Sadan clearly was) of the cultural problematic of modern Jewry and the more or less common sociology of modern Jewish writers, you will want to see the Hebrew enterprise as a parallel undertaking to that of Jewish writers working in Yiddish, German, English, or other languages.

In any event, it is a tricky business to trace analogies and correspondences among these several Jewish literatures for two reasons. First, there are complicating differences, in some ways crucial ones, in the supposedly shared social circumstances of modern Jews. Though both the immigrants to America and the parents of Central European writers like Freud and Kafka were refugees from the *shtetl*, there is a world of difference between, say, Vienna and Prague circa 1910, and New York and Montreal of the same period, and Odessa in 1910 would be still another story. Jewish families no doubt resemble each other more than they do black American families or British middle class families, but that hardly means that one can speak of a dependably stable constellation of the Jewish family from Minsk to Minneapolis. Even if one could, there remains a second difficulty: imaginative writers, including those committed to a realist agenda, never simply "reflect" the social conditions of their upbringing but variously refract them through the dense and irregular medium of their own preoccupations, sensibility, and expressive aims. Thus, there is an unpredictable dialectic between the undeniable social matrix of literature and the stubborn individuality of the particular writer's work. That dialectic is bound to complicate the instructive but risky task of following connections between Hebrew writers and other modern Jewish writers.

To consider a central instance, what happens in the fictional representation of the family? Fiction is informed by an impulse to generalize, to symbolize, to make the particular somehow exemplary – and often, I would add, exemplary of aspects of existence by no means limited to social institutions and their consequences in individual lives. Thus, a social institution appearing in a fictional text may be neither a laboratory specimen of a general condition nor an individual case study, though it may often oscillate over some ambiguous middle ground between the two. Recall the famous first sentence of *Anna Karenina*: "Happy families are all alike; every unhappy family is unhappy in its own way." It is of course the second clause that is to be the subject of Tolstoy's novel, as it is, indeed, of every novel, for about happy families there is hardly anything to be narrated. But that second clause operates in an odd, unsettling state of tension with the first clause, as if somehow the novel could make sense of the peculiarity of the particular only by setting it against the background of what is universally shared. As we read on, we discover that the Karenins and the Oblonskys are wretchedly unhappy each in their own way, but their unhappiness is, after all, also exemplary, just as the eventual happiness of Levin and Kitty is in certain regards decidedly peculiar. The very assertions, then, about what is typical and what is unique may be reversible, and that instability of the seemingly typical characterizes most fictional expressions of social realities.

In discussing the Jewish family in literature, the question we must ask is what writers make of the family rather than what picture of the actual family we can build by scrutinizing their texts. It does not, for example, seem to me feasible to draw valid general inferences about what has happened to the Jewish family in America by canvassing a sampling of American Jewish novels. An instructive failed project of this sort is an essay published some years ago on the Jewish mother in contemporary American fiction by the neo-Orthodox critic, Harold Fisch. According to Fisch, in the traditional Jewish family the father was endowed with an aura of authority by virtue of the domestic religious system over which he presided. Once belief was eroded and the bonds of observance went slack, the father became a displaced person, powerless, pathetic, figuratively or literally constipated, while the possessive, overbearing, guilt-inducing mother now reigned supreme. In this way, the notorious Jewish mother of American fiction of the sixties was the clear symptom of a social pathology of posttraditional Jewish life.

Like most sweeping sociological generalizations, there is a grain of truth in all of this, but I am skeptical about whether it is the sort of truth that would stand the test of statistical analysis. If this is more or less the image we get of Jewish mothers and fathers in, say, the early novels of Philip Roth, we are surely entitled to ask how much of this is typical of second-generation families of the Jewish middle class in the urban centers of the Northeast, how much is attributable to the personal experience of Philip Roth, and how much to the generic and formal necessities of the kind of fiction he is writing, that is, a variety of erotic *Bildungsroman* in which the plot of attempted self-discovery through exogamous union needs the possessive, rasping, anaphrodisiac mother as an obstacle to overcome.

What I am proposing to do here, then, is to offer not an overview of the modern Jewish family through the evidence of literary texts but rather some instances of how certain elements of the sociology of the modern Jewish family have been transmuted in fiction. I will focus on three major figures working in three different languages: Franz Kafka, S. Y. Agnon, and Saul Bellow. The three can by no means suggest all that has been made by modern writers of the Jewish family, but they may indicate three cardinal points on the map of possibilities. I will proceed in chronological order, though I do not mean to imply a necessary historical chronology; the sequence will be from fathers to mothers to cousins.

Among the writings of Kafka, the primary document on his relation to the family is the *Letter to His Father*, a text of some twenty thousand words that he wrote in November 1919, just five years before his death, and that was never delivered to its addressee. Precisely because the *Letter to His Father* is not a work of fiction, it offers an illuminating instance of how the materials of life are transformed when they are turned into fiction.

The letter is based on a ghastly contradiction that seems quite out of control for the writer (unlike his fiction, where contradictions are held in fiercely artful control). Intended as a gesture of reconciliation and, in a peculiar way, as an expression of frustrated filial love, it is one of the most terrible indictments imaginable of a father by his son. The son repeatedly confesses his own weakness, his impotence, his abiding sense of guilt, but through anecdote and analysis he makes painfully clear how the father is responsible for the catastrophe of his son's character. This is a lifelong contest between hopeless unequals: "we were so different and in our difference so dangerous to each other that if anyone had tried to calculate in advance how I, the slowly developing child, and you, the full-grown man, would stand to each other, he could have assumed that you would simply trample me underfoot so that nothing was left of me." The perception of the father is an infantile one that seems never to have been altered by the growth of little Franz to adult proportions: "Sometimes I imagine the map of the world spread out and you stretched diagonally across it. And I feel as if I could consider living in only those regions that either are not covered by you or are not within your reach."

To what extent does any of this reflect the general condition of the Jewish bourgeois family in the Austro-Hungarian empire around the turn of the century? (These are the same time and geographical sphere, by the way, as those of Agnon's formative years, the Galician Agnon being just seven years Kafka's junior, though his greatest achievements would occur in the quarter-century after the death of his Czech counterpart.) Hermann Kafka, at least on the evidence of his son's letter, was an overbearing bully, a vulgarian, a monster of egotism, and in his modest way something of a sadist. Fortunately, none of these attributes can be referred to the sociology of the Jewish family. Kafka himself, however, does touch on certain notes of social generalization in the letter, and these demonstrate how the fateful peculiarities of individual character may be significantly reinforced by certain elements of shared cultural experience.

The senior Kafka, as part of the vast immigration from *shtetl* to city that took place in Central Europe at this time, was pre-eminently a self-made man, and the force of self-assertion of this successful new member of the urban mercantile class was of a piece with his penchant for domination within the family: "You had worked your way so far up by your own energies alone, and as a result you had unbounded confidence in your opinion." Hermann Kafka had jettisoned the pious practice of the world of his childhood, retaining only a kind of tenuous and intermittent nostalgia for it that was expressed in little more than perfunctory attendance at synagogue services four times a year. His son of course sensed the emptiness of this vestigial reflex of observance, and in the letter he imagines that, had the religious situation been different, "we might have found each other in Judaism."

Kafka himself stresses the typicality of the predicament: "The whole thing is, of course, no isolated phenomenon. It was much the same with a large section of this transitional generation of Jews, which had migrated from the still comparatively devout countryside to the cities." In the absence of authoritative tradition, the assertive father becomes an absolute arbitrary authority with all the force of the most punitive aspects of the God of tradition. (One sees here that Harold Fisch's argument about the erosion of faith and the obtrusion of Jewish mothers can easily be turned the other way to explain overbearing fathers.) Kafka summarizes this displacement in a single brief statement about his upbringing: "But for me as a child everything you called out at me was positively a heavenly commandment [*Himmelsgebot*]." The child, and the man-child after him, is forever at the foot of a towering Sinai, hearing the words hurled down at him in thunder, but the words frequently change, attach themselves to absurd or trivial objects, and are flagrantly violated by the very person who pronounces them.

In the *Letter to His Father*, all this amounts to an anguished account of the genesis of a neurosis, though, as I have just indicated, there is a sociological as well as a characterological component in the family situation that contributes to the inner crippling of the son. In Kafka's fiction, these same materials are transformed into haunting narrative explorations of the dynamics of living in families, living under political and spiritual constraint, living under the pressure of eternally elusive moral imperatives. That is why we read *The Trial*, *The Castle*, and the major short stories as great fictions of our dark times, not merely as the record of a cluster of obsessions. What the stories and novels do is to effect a symbolic reconfiguration of the family, the author using his own experience of the posttraditional Jewish family matrix as the means to represent existence under a strictly lawlike, perhaps lawless, authority. Let me try to illustrate this process by some brief comments on the three remarkable stories, all of them written between 1912 and 1914, that constitute a kind of unintended small trilogy on the fate of filiation: "The Judgment," "The Metamorphosis," and "In the Penal Colony."

"The Judgment" is the starkest, the most claustral, of these three grim tales. The power of the story derives precisely from the fact that all of reality has been stripped down to nothing more than the relation between the father and his son, Georg Bendermann. The only scene for action outside the dark rooms where the two Bendermanns live is the bridge from which Georg will fling himself at the end. There are only two other human figures, both of whom exist at the periphery of this world. One is a friend in Russia, who is variously a figment of Georg Bendermann's imagination, an alter ego, a bone of contention between father and son, and an alternative image of a son for Bendermann senior. The other figure in the background is Georg's putative fiancée.

Now, one of the recurrent topics of the *Letter to His Father* is Franz Kafka's inability to marry, which he attributes to his sense of devastating weakness vis-à-vis the powerful paterfamilias whose role he cannot hope to emulate, whose place he does not dare usurp. In the letter, this notion has the status of a symptom and the tonality of a tormented whine. Translated into the narrative invention of "The Judgment," the idea picks up archetypal force: the conflict between the two Bendermanns becomes the immemorial conflict between father and son in which every attempt of the son to take a sexual partner is construed as a betrayal, a thinly veiled project to displace the father and possess a surrogate of the mother. "Because . . . the nasty creature," thunders Bendermann *père*, referring to the fiancée, "lifted her skirts . . . you made up to her, and in order to make free with her undisturbed you have disgraced your mother's memory, betrayed your friend, and stuck your father in bed so he can't move."

The intuitive rightness of invented detail in this symbolic reconfiguration of the family is uncanny: the thigh wound laid bare by the father, which suggests both threatened castration and past prowess in battle; the fact that the father, through the strength of his claimed insight into the son's motives, suddenly grows "radiant" and is able to rise powerfully from bed. The final stroke of the story, a paternal death sentence that the son finds irresistible, is at once the most fantastic and the most symbolically resonant moment of the tale: it carries us back far beyond the Jewish bourgeois familial setting of the Kafkas of

Prague into an archaic shadow world of absolute patriarchal authority where the self-assertive impulse of the young is crushed with savage force.

In "The Metamorphosis," the stroke of fantasy occurs at the very beginning, in the famous first sentence that announces Gregor Samsa's transformation into a gigantic insect. Everything thereafter in the novella follows with a harshly realistic logic from that initial fantastic fact. The sense of unworthiness, of rejection, that Kafka articulates in the *Letter to His Father* is startlingly objectified by this conversion of man into dung beetle – a pariah within the family, an object of embarrassment and loathing, and an insuperable obstacle to normal family existence.

The family as institution is more clearly the central focus of this story than of the other two I am considering. Although the trappings of contemporary urban life – the cramped apartment, the economic endeavors of Gregor and his father – are in evidence, this does not finally seem a "representation" of the early twentieth-century bourgeois family but rather a narrative study of the delicate hydraulic system of the nuclear family as such. Here, too, we have the rivalry of force between father and son, in which as the son becomes weaker (wounded by an apple embedded in his carapace, he is like an "old invalid") the father grows in strength, but that relationship is complicated by the crisscrossing lines of connection among all four members of the family. The crippled son futilely seeks refuge from the hostility of the father in the possibility of maternal solicitude; for a while, he imagines that his sister, who is the one given the task of nurturing him, is his secret ally, but this proves a delusion. In the end, it dawns on him that the only way he can serve the family is through his death.

This frightening tale, then, proves to have a kind of happy ending, whatever ironic inferences one might choose to draw about the conclusion. Gregor's death has a redemptive force: with the noisome giant bug at last out of the way, father, mother, and the suddenly blooming daughter can leave the foul atmosphere of their apartment-prison, walk out into the fresh air of spring, think again of action, renewal, and a clean, fresh place to live. To state in shorthand the distance that has been traversed from experience to art, the cramped psychic space of life in the family of Hermann Kafka has been transformed into a scapegoat story – and, alas, all too many families have their scapegoat – where the well-being of the whole is achieved at the cost of the unassimilable individual.

"In the Penal Colony" presents more complications of narrative elaboration than our two other stories, and I can hardly offer a serious interpretation of it in this rapid overview. Like so many Kafka texts, it has been read in very divergent ways: as a theological tale about the transition from the Old Dispensation to the New; as a political fable, uncannily prescient of the concentration-camp universe; as a psychological study of the insidious dialectic between sadism and masochism; and much more. The point I want to stress is that it is precisely through the symbolic reconfiguration of family experience that such a multiplicity of readings becomes possible – because the family, after all, is the matrix of our psychological lives, of our political, moral, and theological imaginings.

In contrast to both "The Judgment" and "The Metamorphosis," no literal family is present here. The setting is a kind of Devil's Island somewhere in the tropics, whose unique system of retribution is the brainchild of a now-deceased Old Commandant. The explorer who comes to witness the operation of the terrible torture machine, explained in such loving detail by the officer in charge of it, provides a zone of mediation and distancing absent in the other two stories: when he pushes off from the shore in his boat at the end, whipping away the oustretched hands of a soldier and a prisoner with a heavy knotted rope, we get a sense that he – and all of us with him – is literally putting behind him the nightmare world of the Old Commandant.

And yet, this distanced, fabulous world of perfectly programmed punishment is fraught with familial energies, energies one sees expressed on a much lower plane of signification in the *Letter to His Father*. The relationship between the Old Commandant and the officer is manifestly one of father and son, and the officer, in attempting, however futilely, to replicate the dead Commandant, is a kind of Hermann Kafka under the aspect of eternity, or at least, under the aspect of political morality. "My guiding principle is this," he tells the explorer, "guilt is never to be doubted." At the end of the story, the failed authoritative father will try to become the submissive son, stripping himself and placing his own body under the teeth of the dreadful Harrow.

The notion of divine commandment, *Himmelsgebot,* which was the young Franz Kafka's sense of his father's words, here undergoes a grotesque transmogrification, for this is a story about supposedly revelatory, indecipherable inscriptions. When the explorer confesses that he can't make out the labyrinthine tracings on the paper the officer shows him, the officer comments, "It's no calligraphy for schoolchildren. It needs to be studied." In the end, the machine that is to inscribe the injunction of justice on the body of the transgressor goes haywire, and the redemptive revelation of the language of the law turns into sheer mayhem.

The three stories, then, mark a course of growing elaboration and imaginative transformation of the familial materials: from the symbolic confessional mode of "The Judgment" to the fantasy and expiative ritual of "The Metamorphosis" to the invented exotic world of "In the Penal Colony," where the writer's personal awareness of an overpowering father and his perception of the displacement of tradition in his own home produce a fable that resonates in multiple registers, leading us to reflect on the failed project of perfect justice, the stubborn human need for punishment, the abuses of political authority, the historical transition from an era of harsh retribution, the breakdown of revelation, and the threat of the indecipherable that subverts any confident use of language.

On the surface, it might seem that the case of the Hebrew writer S. Y. Agnon is incommensurate with that of Kafka, for Agnon's fictional world is so much more varied in topic, genre, and tone. In over sixty years of literary activity, Agnon produced cunningly artful imitations of pious tales, nostalgic reminiscences of his childhood, subtle psychological studies of contemporary types, panoramically realistic novels (though the realism is almost always tinctured with something else), satires, a whole spectrum of symbolic fiction, and also some dreamlike expressionistic stories that in fact have been compared with Kafka. But beneath this variety of literary kinds, one detects a family constellation only a little less obsessive than that encountered in Kafka. For Agnon, it is the looming figure of the mother rather than of the father that constantly overshadows the existence of the son.

In Agnon's case, we know lamentably little about the specific circumstances of the Czaczkes (his original family name) ménage in turn-of-the-century Buczacz, and considering the almost total neglect of serious literary biography by Hebrew scholarship, we are not likely to find out much before the last remaining witnesses will have vanished. But if the actual etiology of Agnon's imagination of the family may be inaccessible, the pattern articulated in his stories and novels is itself eloquent. In Agnon's world of origins, the mother reigns and the father is strangely recessive or actually absent. Occasionally, she is seen as a thinly veiled object of erotic yearning: thus the mother of Yitzhak Kumer, the protagonist of *Just Yesterday* (1945, still untranslated)—he recalls her last lingering kiss and in that recollection recoils in guilt from attachment to another woman; or the mother of Jacob Rechnitz in the symbolic novella *Betrothed* (1943), who is confused in her son's mind with the mother of his fiancée, whom in turn he eerily confounds with her own daughter.

In Agnon's fiction, mothers are powerful either through their own force of will or through the sexual attraction they exert on their sons. *A Simple Story* (1935, available in English), the novel that is Agnon's masterpiece of psychological realism, offers the most clear-cut instance of domination by the mother as against attraction to the mother. Tzirel Hurvitz, a strong-willed, self-assured, grasping shopkeeper—a kind of fictional soul-sister to Hermann Kafka—possesses her son without ever having really nurtured him: she blocks his way to the poor cousin who is the woman he longs for, marries him off, out of social and economic calculation, to a woman he does not want, enlists him despite himself in the family business, and is ultimately responsible for his attempted escape into madness. (These are, let me note, strictly observant Jews, like Agnon's own family: one hardly needs Harold Fisch's thesis of the breakdown of traditional patriarchal authority to explain the baleful eminence in some writers of the Jewish mother.)

As the related fates of Hirshl Hurvitz in *A Simple Story* and Jacob Rechnitz in *Betrothed* suggest, powerful or powerfully desired mothers in Agnon tend to make weak sons, and the passivity, the debility, the impotence of Agnon's male figures have long been observed by critics. This kind of protagonist is prominent as early as *The Hill of Sand* (1919, but based on a story written in 1911, when Agnon was only twenty-three; it is still untranslated), with its touch-me-touch-me-not central character wandering through a labyrinth of castration symbols, and as late as the posthumously published novel *Shira* (1971), the story of a hopelessly blocked scholar alternately mothered by his prematurely aging wife and obsessed by his domineering, elusive, weirdly androgynous mistress.

The examples I have touched on illustrate how Agnon could spin, out of his own obsessive concern with mothers and sons, a long series of variations on a single psychological type, or, if we stress relationship rather than character in these fictions, a series of studies of the psychopathology of erotic life. Nor is the psychopathology of the erotic by any means limited to the overtly modernist phrases of Agnon's writing, as we may infer from the disquieting story of an unconsummated marriage in "The Scribe's Legend" (1919), an ostensibly pious tale where the values of piety are ironically subverted from beginning to end. If, as I argued at the outset, a fictional representation is never just a case study, what is finally most arresting about Agnon's preoccupation with these family materials is his ability to address through them a range of large questions involving the cultural and spiritual predicaments of our century. This is evident, among the works I have already mentioned, in *Just Yesterday*, *Betrothed*, and *Shira*, but I would like to follow a little more closely the move from family to culture and history in another text, the 1951 novella *Edo and Enam*, which I think is one of Agnon's most original symbolic fictions.*

Edo and Enam is a story about the mystique of archeology and the quest after lost civilizations, and as such would not at first blush seem

---

* Both *Betrothed* and *Edo and Enam* are available in English (*Two Tales*, Schocken).

to have a great deal to do with families. A lonely scholar, Dr. Ginath, becomes famous by deciphering the hitherto unknown language of Edo and by publishing the beautiful Enamite hymns, said to stand as the missing link at the very dawn of human history. In the course of the story, it emerges that his source for both the language and the hymns is a somnambulistic woman named Gemulah who has been brought to Jerusalem as a wife from her exotic mountain homeland by Gabriel Gamzu, an antiquarian discoverer of rare books and manuscripts. The symbolism of this strange and evocative tale has been expounded all too many times in Hebrew criticism (and, often, in all too allegorical a manner). Rather than add my own voice to the chorus, I should like to comment on how the familial concerns define the lines of the symbolic picture, give it coherence and dimension.

The contemporary world of *Edo and Enam* is one of epidemic homelessness, where houses are simply unavailable, or are broken into, or are threatened with destruction. The theme of the destroyed house is pervasive in Agnon's fiction, but here it is correlated with the theme of disrupted conjugality. The paradigm is provided in an anecdote about a certain Günther and his bride who have been married for over a year but, unable to find an apartment, live in separate rented rooms, meet at bus stops and park benches, and, one concludes, have had no opportunity to consummate their union. Near the end of the story, we learn that the marriage between Gemulah and Gamzu is also unconsummated: "I am no married woman," Gemulah proclaims to Ginath when the two are discovered together by Gamzu, "ask him if he has ever beheld my naked flesh." Not even adultery is fulfilled: Ginath's relation to Gemulah, as much as she passionately longs for another order of intimacy, is the cool connection of self-interested amanuensis to informant. As for the Greifenbachs, the couple in whose home Ginath lives, there are no indications in the story about their conjugal behavior, but, after ten years of marriage, their union remains without offspring. Finally, the narrator himself, though a husband and father, is separated from his wife and children during the main time sequence of the story and so participates, albeit temporarily, in the general pattern of disrupted conjugality.

What has happened, in short, is that the psychological theme of the weak son, erotically impaired by Oedipal guilt or by maternal domination, has been projected here onto a global scale and translated into nonpsychological terms. It is a pre-eminent instance of what I referred to in the case of Kafka as the symbolic reconfiguration of family materials. The novella gives us a world of ineffectual males, either incapable of or unwilling to achieve conjugal consummation. In the thematic confrontation of modernity and the archaic, this universal slackening of the sexual bond serves as an apt image of a culture that has lost its élan, its sense of direction and purpose, its faith in its capacity for self-perpetuation.

Against this contemporary panorama of failed relations between the sexes, the story offers two ironically unattainable alternatives, one mythic and the other archaic. In the long dialogues between Gamzu and the narrator, mention is made a couple of times of the perfect conjunction between male and female in the heavenly constellations, or, according to the Kabbalah, between the angels of the *Shekhinah*, the female aspect of the Godhead, and the angels of the *Kudsha Brikh Hu*, the male aspect of the Godhead. In a still more pointed antithesis to the flaccid males of the contemporary scene, Gemulah's archaic world is marked by a practice in which the suitor, emulating the biblical story of the seizure of the young women of the tribe of Benjamin, must forcibly "snatch" his bride from all rivals. The contrast between modern exhaustion or sterility and archaic vitality is emphatically clear.

Edo and Enam, however, is more intriguingly ambiguous than my account of it so far would indicate. In her archaic realm, Gemulah is a nurturing mother (she nurses the injured Gamzu back to health when, blinded, he stumbles into her land); in contemporary Jerusalem, she is, to her husband, alternately an invalid daughter, a dangerous she-demon, and an elusive object of desire. But the most devious ironic turn of the tale is that the whole vision of an archaic realm of vital origins proves to be illusory. The language of origins Gemulah speaks is revealed as a concoction, less language than idiolect, a project of se-

cret intimacy shared solely by daughter and father, from which the exogamous suitor, the male outsider, Gamzu, is excluded.

At the heart of the archaic, then, we discover a kind of incestuous
circularity that generates still another version of sexual exclusion.
Language itself, instead of being anchored in history or, according to
Gamzu's kabbalistic perspective, in the cosmos, is fictive; and the Oedipal aspiration of modern culture to return to the source can attain no
more than the pseudoarchaic, the flirtation with an immemorial vitality proving to be a seduction by death.

What happens in the family, as Agnon perceives it, turns out to be
homologous with what happens in culture, but in the larger arena the
consequences seem more portentous. At the very end of the tale, the
narrator tells us that after death, a writer's soul shines out in his work
for anyone with eyes to "make use of its light." This presumably will
be the case with Ginath's publications. But, remembering the ultimately fictive basis of Ginath's discoveries, the deceptive lunar lumi-
nosities with which they are associated, we may also recall an earlier
remark by the narrator about the alluring light of the moon: "Happy is
he who makes use of its light and comes to no harm."

The family in the fiction of Saul Bellow unsettles the nice symmetry of our instances from Kafka and Agnon and so provides a salutary
reminder that there are very different possibilities for turning perceptions of the family to literary purposes. The crucial distinction between Bellow and the two earlier writers is that he is chiefly interested in the extended family, not in the nuclear family. Although he
began his career in the forties with *Dangling Man* in a stark modernist
mode (Dostoevsky-*cum*-Kafka), from the early fifties onward his novels and stories have encompassed not isolated individuals and over-
mastering parents but a welter of disparate, squabbling, ambivalently
loving siblings, uncles and aunts, cousins near and distant.

This attraction to familial sprawl is inseparable from the zest, the
panoramic sweep, and the element of formal looseness in Bellow's fiction. Nothing he has written exhibits the tightness, the inexorability
of "In the Penal Colony" or *Edo and Enam*, but it may well be that

such formal rigor in fiction is dependent upon the imaginative concentration on the tight four-square zone of the nuclear family, and any reaching beyond those limits entails a certain untidiness. Bellow himself seems perfectly aware of the opposition in this regard between his work and that of the moderns. In his recent story "Cousins" (from which I will draw all my examples), the narrator, Ijah Brodsky, reports his ex-wife as having explained his fascination with collateral relatives in the following terms: "Her opinion was that through the cousins . . . I indulged my taste for the easier effects. I lacked true modern severity. Maybe she believed that I satisfied an artist's needs by visits to old galleries, walking through museums of beauty, happy with the charms of kinship, quite contented with painted relics, not tough enough for rapture in its strongest forms, not purified by nihilistic fire." In modernists like Kafka and Agnon, one indeed sees true modern severity, the purging fires of nihilism. Bellow at his best offers a more human warmth, and instead of the intensities of rapture, a compound of wry amusement, curiosity, puzzlement, and compassion.

As fiction moves from the nuclear family to the larger network of relatives, the whole enterprise of symbolic reconfiguration is set aside. There is nothing symbolic about Bellow's cousins and aunts and uncles, no implication of multiple registers of meaning. The Jewish immigrant extended family draws him because it offers such a splendid sampling of human variety, and it is the extravagant particularity of individual character that engages him. But the simile Ijah Brodsky tries on for size, of visiting old galleries, undersells his own and his author's activity as a cousin-watcher, for the impulse is anthropological, in the older, philosophical sense of the term and therefore also ultimately metaphysical.

In the story "Cousins," the language of zoology and, in particular, of evolutionary theory abounds in the characterizations of the relatives: species, forms of life, extinct types, kinds of creatures, and so forth. What range of possibilities for humanity is manifest in these individual figures, known more or less intimately as members of the same family, belonging, as the narrator notes, "to the same genetic pool, with a certain difference in scale"? At one point, Brodsky is led to speculate — and it is a notion that underlies a good deal of Bellow's fiction — that each human being is born with something that deserves to be called an original self, not reducible to common denominators, not explicable through general patterns and external determinants. That would provide a metaphysical warrant for the cognitive seriousness of Bellow's scrutiny of disparate individuals in his fiction: "The seams open, the bonds dissolve, and the untenability of existence releases you back to the original self. Then you are free to look for real being under the debris of modern ideas, and in a magical trance, if you like, or with a lucidity altogether different from the lucidity of *approved* types of knowledge."

What does this enterprise of trying to fathom human variety through collateral relatives have to do with the Jewish family? It is a commonplace that in Western urban societies the extended family has long been in a state of dissolution, and it is obvious that such vestigial forms of it as persist are by no means limited to Jews. Nevertheless, Bellow has his Ijah Brodsky propose that in Jews the corrosive effects of modernization, the devastation of genocide, have produced a certain instinct of reversion to the premodern familial system: "Jewish consanguinity — a special phenomenon, an archaism of which the Jews, until the present century stopped them, were in the course of divesting themselves. The world as it was dissolving apparently collapsed on top of them, and the divestiture could not continue." It is hard to say whether statistical evidence could be mustered to support this assertion, but it does seem to have an intuitive rightness. The Jewish family, like other kinds of family, is inevitably flung out to all points of the compass in the centrifuge of contemporary life, yet one may detect surprising tugs back to the center, perhaps especially over the last decade, as we enter the second generation after that most terrible collapse of the modern world on the Jewish people.

In any case, the literary treatment of the family, as I have been arguing all along, has very little to do with statistics because the writer does not report social institutions but picks up hints from them which he imaginatively elaborates into a certain vision of human possibilities or, we might add, of impossibilities. When the terms the writer works with are drawn from the tightly looped psychosexual circuits of the nuclear family, what he does in one way or another is to derive from the family a defining model of relations between man and woman, strong and weak, old and young, man and God, individual and authority, nature and culture, present and past. I am not enough of a determinist to believe that everything the writer sees is distorted into the image of the family but we do, after all, internalize our childhood families, and that predisposes us to see things in a certain way, to integrate them according to certain patterns, perhaps at times even to glimpse underlying principles that might otherwise escape us. The extended family, by contrast, as the example of Bellow suggests, offers immediate access to the endless heterogeneity of human types.

The bulging familial grab bag of Bellow's story – hoodlum, lawyer, businessman, cabdriving philosopher, vulgarian, aesthete, introvert, female powerhouse – is something many of us experience in our own extended families. The fact that Bellow chooses to begin his catalogue with a criminal is instructive. For the law-abiding citizen, the criminal may often seem alien, someone who has stepped to the other side of a fatal dividing line; but the criminal in the family confronts us with kinship, reminds us that this, too, is a permutation of the human stuff we are made of, and in these physical lineaments we are faced with hints of ourselves.

If, as I have intimated, there is some complicated linkage between the nuclear family and symbolism, there would seem to be a connection between the extended family and what we call realism in fiction. This is not to suggest that the great realists deal only with the extended family (Zola often does, Dickens usually does not), but rather that they typically show the nuclear family to be implicated in larger familial and social contexts. By contrast, the creators of modern symbolic fiction conjure with an enclosed, imploded nuclear family.

The two modes of fiction, to be sure, rarely exist as pure entities and can combine in a variety of ways; but for our present purpose, I would define realism as the fictional invention, based on close observation, of people whose principal interest for us is the peculiar heft of their individuality, not their capacity to serve as conduits to some higher plane of signification. The generalizing impulse of fictional mimesis is in this case more implicit than explicit, operating mainly in that pondering of divergent human possibility to which we are invited. "Human absorption in faces, deeds, bodies, drew me toward metaphysics," Bellow has his Ijah Brodsky say.

The Jewish family is not exactly "portrayed" in Bellow's fiction, but it provides him a special opening for contemplating through particulars humanity at large. The realist and the symbolist, then, arrive at the threshold of metaphysics by very different routes. But it is there, finally, that they both bring their familial concerns, for what the imaginative writer seeks to uncover in the recesses of family life is not a sociological schema but the secret hints of meaning about what we are and where we are headed.

Do language and literary tradition make a difference in any of these fictional treatments of the family? Perhaps, though the only safe generalizations are those that pertain to the peculiar relation to their respective languages of these three individual writers. Bellow is the one who is most completely at home in a vernacular as he writes. His thoroughly American prose is linked with his gift for vivid mimetic dialogue: this zestful ease with the living language may itself encourage him to look at his specimens of the family menagerie realistically as sharp and variegated manifestations of individuality, realizing themselves in their own distinctive words and enlivened by the tonally related words of the narrator. Kafka famously wrote with a sense of inner distance—a certain ineradicable foreignness—from the German language that was his medium. This peculiar sense, which he may well exaggerate in some of the assertions in his letters, for the most part leads him to steer clear of the colloquial register of the language on the one side and its layered historical associations on the other, and to work instead with a kind of impersonal middle diction. That orientation toward his linguistic medium is aptly suited to, and may have helped promote, the universalizing and anthropologically or spiritually symbolic cast of his fiction.

Agnon's linguistic vehicle is the oddest of the three, and can justifiably be seen as the last, modernist turn of the screw of the peculiar literary history of Hebrew before it became once again a vernacular. An aggressively stylized Hebrew, its dominant tonalities are those of the language of the early rabbis, historically removed from Agnon and from many of the pressing concerns of his fiction by a millennium and a half. This archaic language introduces an implicitly ironic distancing in Agnon's modernist stories and novels that has a loose kinship with Kafka. But in sharp contrast to Kafka's German, Agnon's Hebrew is an intricate echo chamber, constantly and deviously recapitulating the literary and theological history of the language as he deploys it. Symbolic reconfiguration of familial and other materials in his fiction is also a repeated interrogation of the values of the present through those of the past, and vice versa. Ecclesiastes and the Book of Judges, medieval Hebrew poetry and the Zohar, resonate weirdly through Israel in the age of archeological discovery, which is the setting of *Edo and Enam*. Of course, such a process of highly charged intertextuality is by no means unique to Hebrew, but it finds an unusually congenial medium in the long literary tradition of Hebrew. An urgent, often surprising dialogue between distant eras, extending to the microscopic articulations of the text, was a distinctive feature of Hebrew literary expression, at least through the middle decades of this century, and even as we approach the century's end, there is at least some evidence in current Hebrew writing, from the poetry of Yehuda Amichai to the avant-garde novels of Yoel Hoffman, that the millennia-long dialogue is far from done.

Index

ROBERT ALTER is Class of 1937 Professor of Hebrew and Comparative Literature at the University of California at Berkeley. He is author of, among other works, *Necessary Angels: Tradition and Modernity in Kafka, Benjamin, and Scholem* and *The Pleasures of Reading in an Ideological Age.*